School Counselor
Leadership

AN ESSENTIAL PRACTICE

By Anita Young, Ph.D., and
Marcy Miller-Kneale

An ASCA National Model® Publication

AMERICAN
SCHOOL
COUNSELOR
ASSOCIATION

ISBN 978-1-929289-39-4

The American School Counselor Association (ASCA) supports school counselors' efforts to help students focus on academic, personal/social and career development so they achieve success in school and are prepared to lead fulfilling lives as responsible members of society. ASCA provides professional development, publications and other resources, research and advocacy to professional school counselors around the globe. For more information visit *www.schoolcounselor.org*.

Table of Contents

Introduction

The identification of individual leadership characteristics and the presence of effective leadership practices are essential for the implementation of sustainable comprehensive school counseling programs. However, school counselors must also be willing to become competent leaders. Reflecting on current leadership beliefs and seeking training opportunities can be the first step for graduate students and practicing school counselors to develop the capacity necessary to expand their professional leadership scope of practice. This book highlights the current school counseling leadership landscape, encourages individual and collaborative reflection, explores leadership models of influence, examines applicable leadership characteristics and practices, and provides examples with reproducible templates for school counselors and school counselor supervisors.

CHAPTER 1

Beliefs: The Cornerstone of Leadership

"A man is but the product of his thoughts – what he thinks he becomes."
Mohandas Gandhi

LEADERSHIP BELIEFS

The ASCA National Model themes of advocacy, collaboration and systemic change integrate leadership to various degrees. We believe leadership may be the essential practice needed to mobilize comprehensive school counseling program implementation. Working as a school counselor leader requires moving beyond transformative school counseling roles to initiating schoolwide or districtwide school counseling systemic strategies and being present at the decision-making tables. The ASCA National Model also emphasizes the alignment of the school counseling vision and mission statement with the instructional mission to ground a data-driven comprehensive school counseling program, based on the fundamental belief that the purpose of school counseling is to advance student learning and enhance the quality of education for all students.

Our beliefs about students drive our actions (ASCA, 2012; Education Trust, 1997; Erford, 2011; Grenny & Patterson, 2013; Young & King, 2002). Examining beliefs is an important consideration to operationally define school counselor leadership; drive interactions with parents, teachers and administrators; and initiate needed programs and services. Moreover, school counselor leaders should be able to clearly articulate the rationale for the school counseling vision based on philosophical beliefs about student learning. As a school counselor leader, your beliefs should be the foundation of your guiding leadership ideals and principles that have an impact on change (Baker & Gerler, 2008).

Leadership Beliefs Reflective Activity

To begin the process of self-reflection, complete the leadership beliefs reflective activity. First, drawing from your beliefs, think about the characteristics you believe are essential for effective leaders to demonstrate. List them on the leadership mapping graph (Figure 1.1). Next, respond to the three Leadership Beliefs Reflective Activity Questions. Finally, discuss your responses with a colleague.

Leadership Mapping Graph (Figure 1.1)

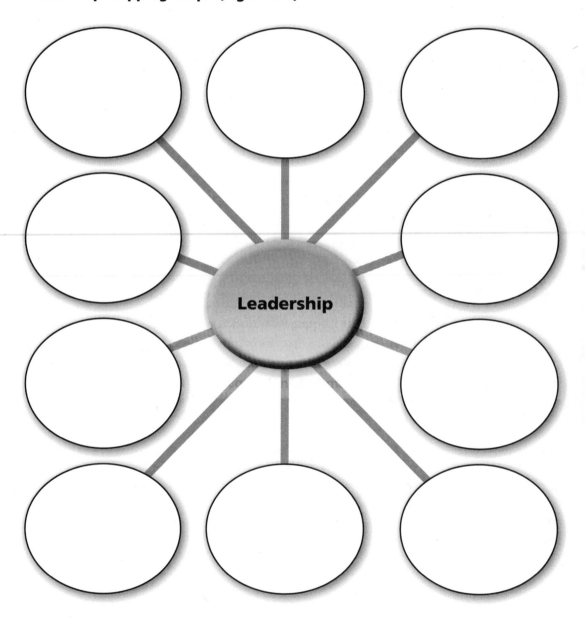

Leadership Beliefs Reflective Activity Questions

Use the leadership mapping graph as your guide. Reflect on and share three leadership characteristics you believe you possess.

1.

2.

3.

In what ways are the personal characteristics you listed congruent or incongruent with your beliefs about essential leadership characteristics?

1.

2.

3.

What barriers are preventing you from practicing the characteristics you believe are essential for leaders?

1.

2.

3.

VISIONARY LEADERSHIP

Having a vision is often considered a characteristic for effective leadership. A vision provides purpose, charts a course for the future and helps identify goals (Bennis, 2003; Dufour, Dufour, Eaker, & Many, 2010; Levin, 2000; Reeves, 2006). The vision is founded on a leader's beliefs and, in the case of schools, beliefs about student learning and the ability to achieve. When a leader articulates the vision, followers are motivated to accomplish goals and work cohesively with a shared purpose. Blanchard (2007, p. 22) believes, "A vision builds trust, collaboration, interdependence, motivation and mutual responsibility for success." Visionary leaders think systemically to accomplish goals.

ACTIVITY: **Vision Reflective Activity**

Continue to use the Leadership Mapping Graph (Figure 1.1) to guide the completion of this activity. In what ways do the leadership characteristics that you identified align with your school counseling vision? Principal's vision?

Figure 1.2

	School Counseling (Program) Vision	Principal's (School) Vision
1		
2		
3		

The school counseling vision statement charts the course for the delivery of equitable programs and services that close achievement and opportunity gaps. It is the school counseling leader's responsibility to ensure alignment with the principal's instructional vision (Dahir & Stone, 2012), inspire others to follow, monitor the implementation of the vision through goal-setting and outcome data and share the vision with stakeholders (Hanson & Stone, 2002; Kose, 2011; Kaffenberger & Young, 2013). School counselor leaders should chart the course for the school counseling program, but they should also establish an individual professional leadership vision.

TEMPLATE **School Counselor Leadership Visionary Planning Template**

Use the school counselor leadership visionary planning template to draft and chart your professional vision (Figure 1.3).

School Counselor Leadership Visionary Planning Template (Figure 1.3)

Name: Date:

What is the school counseling program vision for the current school year?

How does the vision change in three years? Five years?

Does the school counseling program vision align with ASCA's recommendations for an effective vision statement (ASCA, 2012, p. 24)? Circle: Yes or No. If no, explain.

What are the big-picture needs for the students in my building? District?

Does the school counseling vision address the big-picture needs?

How is your individual professional vision congruent with the school counseling program vision?

REFERENCES

American School Counselor Association (2012). *The ASCA National Model: A framework for school counseling programs* (3rd ed.). Alexandria, VA: Author.

Baker, S. B., & Gerler, E. R. (2008). *School counseling for the twenty-first century* (5th ed.). Upper Saddle River, NJ: Pearson Merrill/Prentice Hall.

Bennis, W. (2003). *On becoming a leader.* New York: Basic Books.

Blanchard, K. (2007). *Leading at a higher level: Blanchard on leadership and creating high performing organizations.* Upper Saddle River, NJ: Prentice Hall.

Dahir, C. A., & Stone, C. B. (2012). *The transformed school counselor* (2nd ed.). Belmont, CA: Brooks/Cole.

Dufour, R., Dufour, R., Eaker, R., & Many, T. (2010). *Learning by doing: A handbook for professional learning communities at work* (3rd ed). Bloomington IN: Solution Tree Press.

Education Trust (1997). *The national guidance and counseling reform program.* Washington, DC: Author.

Erford, B. T. (2011). *Transforming the school counseling profession* (3rd ed). Upper Saddle, NJ: Merrill Prentice Hall.

Hanson, C., & Stone, C. B. (2002). Recruiting leaders to transform school counseling. *Theory into Practice, 41,* 163-168.

Kaffenberger, C. & Young, A. (2013). *Making data work* (3rd ed.). Alexandria, VA: American School Counselor Association.

Kose, B. W. (2011). Developing a transformative school vision: Lessons from peer-nominated principals. *Education and Urban Society, 43,* 119-136.

Levin, I. M. (2000). Vision revisited: Telling the story of the future. *The Journal of Applied Behavioral Science. 36,* 91-107.

Grenny, J., & Patterson, K. Maxfield (2013). *Influencer: The power to change anything* (2nd ed.). New York: McGraw-Hill.

Reeves, D. B., (2006). *The learning leader.* Alexandria, VA: Association for Supervision and Curriculum Development.

Young, P., & King, M. B. (2002). Principal leadership for professional development to build school capacity. *Educational Administration Quarterly, 38,* 5, 643-670.

CHAPTER 2

A Convergent Framework of the School Counseling Leadership Landscape

"Leaders do not avoid, repress or deny conflict but rather see it as an opportunity."
Warren Bennis

The critical need to train school counseling graduate students to demonstrate leadership capacity and the call to action for school counselors to be leaders has been established (ASCA, 2012; CACREP, 2009; DeVoss & Andrews (2006); Dollarhide, Gibson, & Saginak, 2008; Dollarhide & Lemberger, 2006; Education Trust, 1996; House & Hayes, 2002; Hanson & Stone, 2002; Janson, Stone, & Clark, 2009; NOSCA, 2011; Sink, 2009; Trusty & Brown; 2005). Yet, the relationship among school counseling and education reform, data and accountability, closing achievement gaps and seeking links to systemic changes via evidence-based research remains an ongoing focus. Many school counselors may find themselves questioning the significance of their previous training and the existence of their leadership practices. They may even ponder their ability to provide appropriate services that produce systemic change.

In this chapter, we explore the school counseling leadership landscape in the current age of accountability and education reform. Building school counselor leadership capacity can begin with pre-service training for graduate students and professional development training for school counselor practitioners that emphasizes leadership as a critical practice for the design and implementation of comprehensive school counseling programs. In an attempt to redirect pre-service training, counselor educators are restructuring curricula and preparing prospective school counselors to be leaders that effect change. The Council for Accreditation of Counseling and Related Education Programs (CACREP) emphasizes the importance of teaching effective leadership skills and practices to graduate students through requirements to design, implement and evaluate comprehensive school counseling programs (CACREP, 2009). School counseling graduate students are also taught to plan and design school counseling programs to inform stakeholders, close achievement gaps and promote college access (McDonough, 2004).

At the practitioner level, the National Association for College Admission Counseling's (NACAC) statement on counselor competencies highlights the need for school counselors to serve as "leaders by demonstrating advocacy and leadership in advancing the concerns of students" (*http://www.nacacnet.org/about/Governance/Policies/Documents/Counselor Competencies.pdf*). Similarly, the American School Counselor Association (ASCA) acknowledges the importance of leadership by citing experts in the school counseling profession who report school counselor leadership means supporting academic achievement and student development to advance the effectiveness of comprehensive school counseling programs (ASCA, 2012). The ASCA National Model also identifies school counselor leaders as culturally responsive change agents. The Education Trust (1996) emphasizes the increased importance of school counselor leadership by proposing school counselors serve as effective team leaders in school reform, increase student achievement and promote college readiness. The Education Trust National Center for Transforming School Counseling released "Poised to Lead: How School Counselors Can Drive College and Career Readiness" (Hines & Lemons, 2011) to accentuate the influence school counselors bring to the college and career readiness platform. With such convergent emphasis on school counselor leadership, we are left to ponder what more is needed to spur school counselor leadership capacity?

HORIZONTAL AND VERTICAL LEADERSHIP

To answer the question, we propose considering the scope and practice of school counselors from a horizontal and vertical dimension. *Consider horizontal leadership as school counselors leading change efforts within their current role to improve outcomes for all students. School counselors who lead horizontally serve as change agents within their current settings. They lead collaborative efforts with other professionals as well as other preK-16 educators to address systemic issues affecting student success.* Horizontal leaders understand the relationship between the instructional vision and mission of the school and the school counseling program. Examples of horizontal leadership may be exhibited by school counselors who work as the only school counselor in their building or work within school counseling teams. In essence, school counselors at all levels, in all settings, have the capacity to lead horizontally.

Vertical leadership is demonstrated by school counseling professionals serving in supervisory roles. *Vertical leadership incorporates all aspects of horizontal leadership and expands to include a responsibility to develop leadership among the school counselors they supervise. Additionally, vertical leadership requires working collaboratively with stakeholders to secure the necessary resources and training for school counselors to implement and lead comprehensive school counseling programs.* Examples of vertical leadership are lead school counselors, department chairs, building-level school counselor supervisors, district school counseling supervisors and state supervisors.

In chapter three, we suggest an operational definition of school counselor leadership incorporating both horizontal and vertical attributes and practices to mobilize school counselor leadership. The Horizontal and Vertical Worksheet on the next page allows you to personalize and identify your leadership capacity as vertical and horizontal leaders.

Convergent Framework Activity

Use the Horizontal and Vertical Worksheet to identify your horizontal and vertical responsibilities.

Horizontal And Vertical Worksheet (Figure 2.1)

Name:	Date:

How do you characterize you current leadership dimension?
Circle: Horizontal or Vertical

Are there situations in which you exhibit both horizontal and vertical leadership capacity?
Circle: Yes or No
Explain:

What evidence supports your beliefs?
Record your responses below with specific examples.

Leadership Dimension	Examples
Horizontal	
Vertical	

REFERENCES

American School Counselor Association (2012). *The ASCA National Model: A framework for school counseling programs* (3rd ed.). Alexandria, VA: Author.

Council for Accreditation of Counseling and Related Educational Programs, 2009 Standards (2009). http://www.cacrep.org/doc/2009%20Standards%20with%20cover.pdf.

DeVoss, J., & Andrew, M.F. (2006). *School counselors as educational leaders*. Boston, MA: Houghton – Mifflin

Dollarhide, C., Gibson, D., & Saginak, K. (2008). New counselors' leadership efforts in school counseling: Themes from a year-long qualitative study. *Professional School Counseling, 11*(4), 262-271.

Dollarhide, C. T., & Lemberger, M. E. (2006). No child left behind: Implications for school counselors. *Professional School Counseling, 9*, 295-304.

Education Trust (1996). *National initiative to transform school counseling*. Washington, DC: Author.

Hanson, C., & Stone, C. B. (2002). Recruiting leaders to transform school counseling. *Theory into Practice, 41*(3), 163-168.

Hines, P., & Lemon, R. (2011). *Poised to Lead: How School Counselors Can Drive College and Career Readiness*. http://www.edtrust.org/dc/publication/poised-to-lead. Retrieved on February 16, 2013.

House, R. M., & Hayes, R. L. (2002). School counselors: Becoming key players in school reform. *Professional School Counseling, 5*, 249-261.

Janson, C., Stone, C., & Clark, M. A. (2009). Stretching leadership: A distributed perspective for counselor leaders. *Professional School Counseling, 13*, 2, 98-105.

McDonough, P.M. (2004). *Choosing colleges: How social class and school structure opportunity*. Albany, NY: State University of New York Press.

National Association for College Admission Counseling (2012). http://www.nacacnet.org/about/Governance/Policies/Documents/CounselorCompetencies.pdf). Retrieved on January 12, 2013.

National Office for School Counselor Advocacy (2011). http://nosca.collegeboard.org/research-policies/annual-survey. Retrieved on December 2, 2012.

Sink, C., (2009). School counselors as accountability leaders: Another call for action. *Professional School Counseling, 13*, 2, 68-73.

Trusty, J., & Brown, D. (2005). *Designing and leading comprehensive school counseling programs: Promoting student competence and meeting student needs*. Pacific Grove, CA: Thomson Brooks/Cole.

CHAPTER 3

Operationalizing School Counselor Leadership

"*A leader is one who knows the way, goes the way and shows the way.*"
John Maxwell

The term capacity to lead is consistently used throughout this book because we believe all school counselors have the ability to acquire leadership skills and to demonstrate leadership practices (ASCA, 2012; DeVoss & Andrews, 2006; Dollarhide, Gibson, & Saginak, 2008; House & Stone, 2002; Janson, Stone, & Clark, 2009; Lambert, 2002; Mason, 2010; Northouse, 2012; Shillingford & Lambie, 2010).Throughout the chapters, you are encouraged to continue reflecting on your leadership beliefs, examine your current leadership practices and commit to building your individual and collaborative school counselor leadership capacity. In this chapter, we operationally define school counselor leadership, examine leadership characteristics and illustrate practices applicable to the scope and practice of school counselors and relevant to increasing the capacity to lead.

PRINCIPAL/SCHOOL COUNSELOR LEADERSHIP RELATIONSHIP

Without question leadership at the school level begins with the principal, but others such as school counselors, teachers, parents and community members also contribute to making schools conducive for learning. In many ways, school counselors and principals are perhaps best positioned to identify global issues affecting student achievement, and they have distinct and shared leadership responsibilities contributing to a school's climate (Stone & Clark, 2001). For some school counselors, this means re-examining the meaning of leadership.

To increase clarification and promote student achievement, let's take a brief look at the similarities and differences between principal leadership and school counselor leadership practices. Principals ensure all students and staff are provided a safe environment conducive for learning. They guide the pedagogical teaching practices related to student performance, set instructional goals that create a climate for rigorous learning outcomes, promote positive collaborative relationships and model a commitment to continuous improvement (Naleithwood & Richl, 2003). School counselors also identify school counseling program goals, ensuring they are specific, measureable, attainable, results-oriented and time-bound (SMART) goals (ASCA, 2012; Doran, 1981; O'Neill & Conzemius, 2005). School counselors collaborate with stakeholders to build school-family-community partnerships, facilitate classroom lessons and small groups to increase student learning outcomes and advocate for equitable services for all students (Bryan & Henry, 2012; Griffin & Farris, 2010; House & Sears, 2002).

Obviously, the responsibilities of principals and school counselors are unlimited, and it is essential for both parties to communicate with each other to align goals and implement effective practices. The affirmative impact of a principal-school counselor relationship is best illustrated in the national reports, "A Closer Look at the Principal-School Counselor Relationship" and "Enhancing the Principal-School Counselor Relationship Toolkit," by ASCA, the National Office for School Counselor Advocacy and the National Association of Secondary School Principals. As a result of a national survey of approximately 2,300 principals and school counselors, the reports identified communication, respect, collaboration and shared vision as critical elements in the principal-school counselor relationship. Without question, when school counselor leaders, both horizontal and vertical, establish a strong working relationship with their principal, school counselors are better informed about parameters for the school counseling program, and the principal develops an understanding of the role and practice of school counselors (NOSCA, ASCA, & NASSP, 2011).

Clearly, leadership is an assumption for many individuals in the school; therefore, principals cannot be expected to function as the single leader for the school without substantial participation of other educators (Lambert, 2002; Young, Millard, & Miller-Kneale, 2013). The assumption is that school counselor leaders not only need thorough graduate academic preparation and continuing professional development training, they also need exposure to schoolwide and districtwide decisions (Young, 2004). School counselors who actively participate on schoolwide and districtwide decision-making teams help meet one of the most important conditions for improving the capacity to lead – the ability to effect positive change for all students.

School Counselor Leadership Landscape Reflective Activity

Figure 3.1

Consider your current environment and respond to the following questions.

How do you think leadership is shared in most schools? Districts?

How is leadership distributed or shared in your school/district?

How are you part of the decision-making process affecting students in your building or district? If you are not, how can you become a part of the decision-making process?

The capacity to lead begins with the identification of leadership characteristics, skills or practices that operationally define the term and increase clarity (Fraenkel, Wallen, & Hyun 2011). Individuals who demonstrate traditional leadership skills and practices are often characterized as charismatic, intelligent, confident, trustworthy, loyal, insightful, accountable, organized, courageous or even creative (Maxwell, 2002; Northhouse, 2012). Unquestionably, these are characteristics and practices enhancing an individual's capacity to lead and are not exhaustive; yet, in isolation they do not necessarily influence change (DuFour, Dufour, Eaker, & Many, 2010). When coupled with a clearly articulated vision and measurable goals, change begins to occur. This formula has proven successful for world leaders, entrepreneurs in private industry and, to an extent, has influenced the educational arena (Conger & Benjamin, 1999; Fullen, 2001).

Although the aforementioned traditional leadership characteristics and practices may be applicable across professions, examining leadership in schools requires the ability to understand the culture of schools and how schools are uniquely designed to meet the needs of students from diverse backgrounds and environments. Because of the uniqueness, leadership in schools is set apart from traditional ideals of leadership (Fullan, 2001; Hanson & Stone, 2002; Harris & Spillane, 2008; Lambert, 2002; Marzano, 2010; Marzano, 2003; Marzano, Waters, & McNulty, 2005). The capacity to lead in schools necessitates a willingness to respect the opinions of students, maintain flexibility, seek common goals with other stakeholders and collaborate with colleagues.

Northouse (2012) describes leadership as a trait, a skill, ability, a behavior, a relationship and as a "process whereby an individual influences a group of individuals to achieve a common goal" (p. 6). Lambert (2002) refers to leadership and learning as reciprocal. Leadership has also been described as developed through interactions of individuals with a common vision, a term coined as distributed leadership (Harris & Spillane, 2008; Spillane, 2006). Examples of how school counselors practice distributed leadership are:

- presenting professional development training to teachers and parents,
- co-facilitating large group counseling lessons with other educators and
- leading the goal to increase college readiness (Janson, Stone, & Clark, 2009).

Similarly, Shillingford and Lambie (2010) stress school counselor leadership is a key behavior to promote professional identity and minimize role inconsistencies. Young (2012) postulates the need for school counselor leaders to be culturally responsive change agents who are willing to integrate instructional best practices, think outside the box, share in schoolwide decisions and model excellence.

ASSESSING SCHOOL COUNSELOR LEADERSHIP

Although school counselor leadership cannot be confined to a specific characteristic or limited to a particular practice or skill, five characteristics and associated practices are recommended to build school counselor leadership capacity. School counselor leaders may exhibit one or multiple characteristics at various times or situations. The characteristics are:

- resourceful problem-solving,
- systemic collaboration,
- interpersonal influence,
- social justice advocacy,
- professional efficacy.

The characteristics were identified from data collected and disaggregated using the School Counselor Leadership Survey, a psychometric sound instrument developed through a three-study process (Young, 2013). The characteristics were identified as a result of the instrument's factor analysis. Approximately 1,579 participants self-reported current behaviors and practices they exhibited using a seven-point Likert scale ranging from never to always. The participants, a stratified sample of American School Counselor Association school counselors and school counselor supervisors from rural, urban and suburban preK-12 levels, served various student populations. Approximately 23.8 percent of participants self-identified as elementary school counselors, 13.4 percent as middle school counselors, 28.3 percent as high school counselors, 6.8 percent as multilevel school counselors, 5.3 percent as supervisors and 22.4 percent as other. Approximately 30 percent of the participants worked in rural settings, 43.2 percent in suburban settings and 25.8 percent in urban settings.

The first characteristic, resourceful problem-solving (Figure 3.1), identified respondents' ability to secure services and programs needed to improve student achievement. Respondents at all levels indicated compassion as a driving force to solve problems. Findings also suggested the importance of a goal-oriented focus to initiate and implement programs and willingness to secure resources to serve all students. Respondents also self-reported exceeding expectations when assigned a school counseling task. Most apparent was the use of data and accountability strategies as a major catalyst to identify goals and necessary interventions.

ACTIVITY: **Resourceful Problem-Solving Activity**

Use the graphic and information provided about the resourceful problem-solving characteristic to provide examples of your practices (Figure 3.2).

Figure 3.2

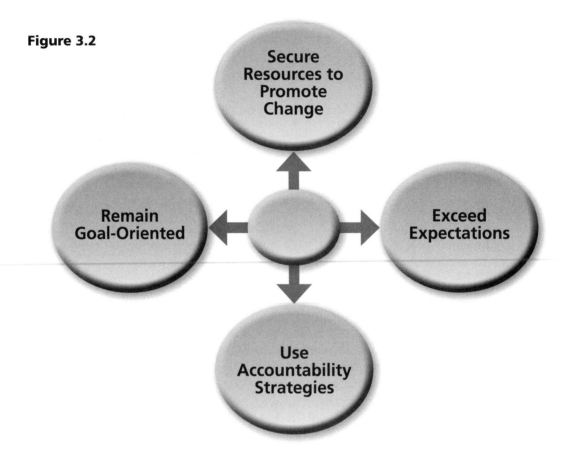

Dimension	Resourceful Problem-Solving Examples
Horizontal	Example: Establish business partnerships to sponsor college field trips for first-generation middle school students in a school with limited financial resources, low parent participation and widening achievement gaps. *Which aspects of the resourceful problem-solving characteristic do you demonstrate? Provide examples.* *1. Secure resources:* *2. Remain goal-oriented:* *3. Use accountability strategies:* *4. Exceed expectations:*
Vertical	Example: Secure funding to train school counselors in the use of data and accountability strategies. *Which aspects of the resourceful problem-solving characteristic do you demonstrate? Provide examples.* *1. Secure resources:* *2. Remain goal-oriented:* *3. Use accountability strategies:* *4. Exceed expectations:*

The second characteristic, systemic collaboration (Figure 3.2), revealed how respondents actively work with stakeholders, implement comprehensive school counseling programs and align services with the instructional vision and mission. Respondents frequently practiced innovativeness. They reported sharing their innovative ideas and encouraging colleagues to share innovative ideas as well. Similarly, schoolwide and district-oriented tasks led to accomplished school program goals. All respondents reported frequent selection to lead schoolwide and districtwide initiatives, committees and councils; however, school counselor supervisors (vertical leaders) reported the highest level of selection (Young, 2013).

ACTIVITY: **Systemic Collaboration Activity**

Use the graphic and information provided about the systemic collaboration characteristic to provide examples of your practices (Figure 3.3).

Figure 3.3

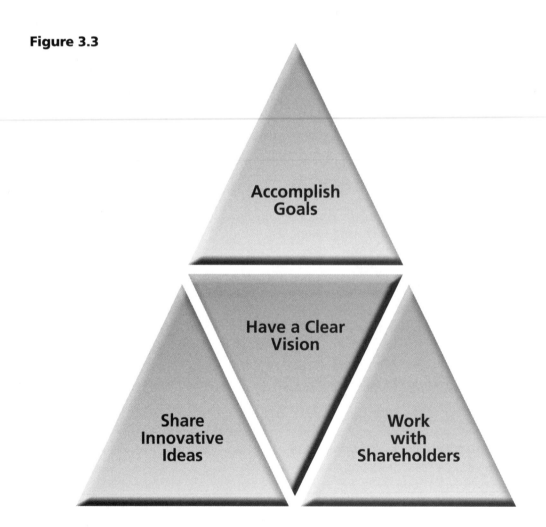

Dimension	Systemic Collaboration Examples
Horizontal	Example: As a result of student outcome data findings, study skills lessons are collaboratively designed and planned with third-grade teachers. *Which aspects of the systemic collaboration characteristic do you demonstrate? Provide examples.* *1. Accomplish goals:* *2. Have a clear vision:* *3. Share innovative ideas:* *4. Work with stakeholders:*
Vertical	Example: Share use-of-time assessments and closing-the-gap reports with principals and other district leaders to minimize non-school-counseling-related duties. *Which aspects of the systemic collaboration characteristic do you demonstrate? Provide examples.* *1. Accomplish goals:* *2. Have a clear vision:* *3. Share innovative ideas:* *4. Work with stakeholders:*

The third characteristic, interpersonal influence (Figure 3.3), encompassed respondents' frequency to promote the school counseling program, motivate followers and accomplish goals that have schoolwide or districtwide impact. Respondents expressed compassion and sincerity as driving forces to serve students and accomplish goals. The ability to navigate through the politics of the school and district and to persuade stakeholder buy-in was notable within this characteristic.

ACTIVITY: **Interpersonal Influence Activity**

Use the graphic and information provided about the interpersonal influence characteristic to provide examples of your practices (Figure 3.4).

Figure 3.4

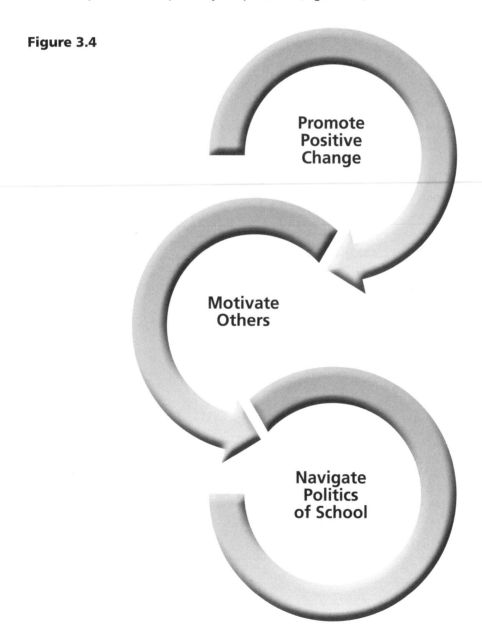

Promote Positive Change

Motivate Others

Navigate Politics of School

Dimension	Interpersonal Influence Examples
Horizontal	Example: Persuade advisory council members to advocate on behalf of the school counseling program. *Which aspects of the interpersonal influence characteristic do you demonstrate? Provide examples.* *1. Promote positive change:* *2. Motivate others:* *3. Navigate politics of school:*
Vertical	Example: Ensure district policies and practices promote access to college- and career-readiness curriculum and activities for all students. *Which aspects of the interpersonal influence characteristic do you demonstrate? Provide examples.* *1. Promote positive change:* *2. Motivate others:* *3. Navigate politics of school:*

Challenging status quo to advocate for all students is a significant variable for the fourth characteristic, social justice advocacy (Figure 3.4). Respondents in this factor expressed a willingness to take risks but not to the extent of crossing ethical boundaries. Advocacy was viewed as a common thread to assume a courageous stance. Respondents also reported a willingness to ask for help when needed to advocate on behalf of students and parents.

ACTIVITY: **Social Justice Advocacy Activity**

Use the graphic and information provided about the social justice characteristic to provide examples of your practices (Figure 3.5).

Figure 3.5

Dimension	Social Justice Advocacy Examples
Horizontal	Example: Question inequitable enrollment patterns by sharing disaggregated data with stakeholders. *Which aspects of the social justice advocacy characteristic do you demonstrate? Provide examples.* *1. Challenge status quo:* *2. Respond to inequities:* *3. Assume a courageous stance:*
Vertical	Example: Ensure district practices allow parents and students to receive information in their home language. *Which aspects of the social justice advocacy characteristic do you demonstrate? Provide examples.* *1. Challenge status quo:* *2. Respond to inequities:* *3. Assume a courageous stance:*

The fifth factor and final characteristic, professional efficacy, exemplified the confidence school counselors and school counselor supervisors believe is needed to effect change. Responses suggest respondents viewed themselves as leaders and change agents, maintained calmness when faced with adversity and believed they have the ability to improve student outcomes.

ACTIVITY: **Professional Efficacy Activity**

Use the graphic and information provided about the professional efficacy characteristic to provide examples of your practices (Figure 3.6).

Figure 3.6

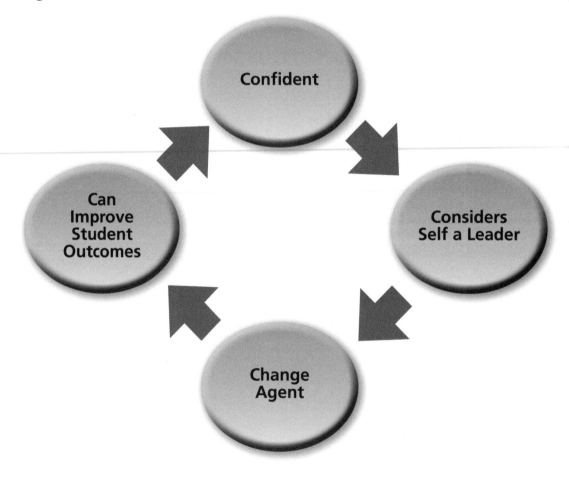

Dimension	Professional Efficacy Examples
Horizontal	Example: Seek and secure a position on the school improvement planning team to improve positive outcomes for all students. *Which aspects of the professional efficacy characteristic do you demonstrate? Provide examples.* *1. Considers self a leader:* *2. Confident:* *3. Change agent:* *4. Improve student outcomes:*
Vertical	Example: Accept the responsibility to mentor and build the leadership capacity of school counselors. *Which aspects of the professional efficacy characteristic do you demonstrate? Provide examples.* *1. Considers self a leader:* *2. Confident:* *3. Change agent:* *4. Improve student outcomes:*

Based on the converging framework of current school counselor leadership literature and findings from the school counselor leadership survey, an operational definition of school counselor leadership characteristics and practices embraces the role of horizontal and vertical school counselor leaders' ability to:

- use multiple strategies and resources to solve problems,
- build partnerships and engage all stakeholders,
- navigate through the politics of systems,
- advocate for equitable services for marginalized and all students with a courageous stance,
- excel in the use of appropriate accountability strategies to challenge status quo,
- persuade colleagues and build consensus,
- identify and accomplish goals with confidence,
- exceed expectations when accomplishing tasks,
- accept the responsibility to lead and
- acquire a leadership mindset (Young, 2013).

ACTIVITY: **School Counselor Leadership Assessment Activity**

Table 3.1 has 10 abbreviated excerpts from the School Counselor Leadership Survey items and the opportunity to assess your current leadership practices. Consider your current practices at your current level when responding. How might your mobilize "no" or "in progress" to "yes."

Table 3.1 School Counselor Leadership Survey (10-item abbreviated excerpt)

Item	Yes	No	In Progress
Accomplish goals with certainty			
Find resources to secure what is needed to improve services for all students			
Advocate for marginalized students			
Share innovative ideas			
Actively work with stakeholders to implement comprehensive school counseling programs			
Remain positive when faced with barriers impeding student success			
Persuade others to gain buy-in			
Accomplish goals that have systemic impact			
Ask for help to advocate on behalf of students and parents			
Have confidence in ability to lead			
Comments: (How to mobilize "no" responses to "yes")			

REFERENCES

American School Counselor Association (2012). *The ASCA National Model: A framework for school counseling programs* (3rd ed.). Alexandria, VA: Author.

Bryan, J., & Henry, L (2012). A model for building school–family–community partnerships: principles and process. *Journal of Counseling Development 90*, 4, 408-420.

Conger, J. A., & Benjamin, B. (1999). *Building leaders: How successful companies develop the next generation.* San Francisco: Jossey-Bass.

DeVoss, J. A., & Andrews, M. F. (2006). *School counselors as educational leaders.* Boston, MA: Houghton Mifflin.

Dollarhide, C., Gibson, D., & Saginak, K. (2008). New counselors' leadership efforts in school counseling: Themes from a year-long qualitative study. *Professional School Counseling, 11*, 4, 262-271.

Doran, G. T. (1981) There's a S.M.A.R.T. way to write management goals and objectives. *Management Review, 70*, 11, 35-36.

Dufour, R., Dufour, R., Eaker, R., & Many, T. (2010). *Learning by doing: A handbook for professional learning communities at work* (3rd ed). Bloomington IN: Solution Tree Press.

Fraenkel, J., Wallen, N., & Hyun, H. (2011). *How to design & evaluate research in education* (8th ed.). Boston, MA: McGraw Hill.

Fullan, M. (2001). *The new meaning of educational change* (3rd ed.). New York: Teachers College Press.

Griffin, D., & Farris, A. (2010). School counselors and collaboration: Finding resources through community asset mapping. *Professional School Counseling 13*, 5, 248-256.

Hanson, C., & Stone, C. B. (2002). Recruiting leaders to transform school counseling. *Theory into Practice, 41*(3), 163-168.

Harris, A., & Spillane, J., (2008). Distributed leadership through the looking glass. *Management In Education, 22*, 31-34.

House, R., & Sears, S. (2002). Preparing school counselors to be leaders and advocates: A critical need in the new millennium. *Theory into Practice, 41*, 154-162.

Janson, C., Stone, C., & Clark, M. A. (2009). Stretching leadership: A distributed perspective for counselor leaders. *Professional School Counseling, 13*, 2, 98-105.

Lambert, L. (2002). A framework for shared leadership. *Educational Leadership, 58*, 8, 37-40.

Naleithwood, K., & Richl, C. (2003). *What we know about successful school leadership.* Philadelphia, PA: National College for School Leadership.

Mason, E. (2010). Leadership practices of school counselors and counseling programs. *NASSP Bulletin, 94*, 4, 274-285.

Marzano, R. (2003). *What works in schools: Translating research into action.* Alexandria, VA: Association for Supervision and Curriculum Development.

Marzano, R. (2010). High expectations for all. *Educational Leadership, 68*, 82-85.

Marzano, R., Waters, T., & McNulty, B. (2005). *School leadership that works: From research to results.* Alexandria, VA: ASCD.

Maxwell, J. C. (2002). *The 17 essential qualities of a team player.* Thomas Nelson: TN

National Office for School Counselor Advocacy, National Association of Secondary School Principals, and American School Counselor Association (2011). A closer look at the principal-counselor relationship. http://media.collegeboard.com/digitalServices/pdf/nosca/a-closer-look_2.pdf. Retrieved on January 16, 2013.

National Office of School Counselor Advocacy, National Association of Secondary Principals, and American School Counselor Association (2011). Principal-counselor relationship toolkit. Retrieved from http://media.collegeboard.com/digitalServices/pdf/nosca/11b_4729_PC_Toolkit_WEB_1 11104.pdf

Northhouse, P. (2012) *Introduction to leadership: Concepts and practice.* Thousand Oaks: CA: SAGE.

O'Neill, J. & Conzemius, A. (2005). *The power of SMART goals: Using goals to improve student learning.* Bloomington, IN: Solution Tree Press.

Shillingford, M. A. & Lambie, G. W. (2010). Contribution of professional school counselors' values and leadership practices to their programmatic service delivery. *Professional School Counseling, 13,* 208-217.

Spillane, J. P. (2006). Distributed leadership. The Educational Forum, 69, 143-150.

Stone, C. B. & Clark, M. A. (2001). School counselors and principals: Partners in support of academic achievement. *NASSP Bulletin, 85,* 46-53.

Young, A. (2004). *Preparing school counselor leaders: The perceptions and practices of transforming school counseling initiative graduates from The Ohio State University.* (Unpublished doctoral dissertation). The Ohio State University, Columbus, OH.

Young, A. (2012). Leadership. In *ASCA National Model: A framework for school counseling programs* (3rd ed.; pp.11-13). Alexandria, VA: American School Counselor Association.

Young, A. (2013). *Assessing school counselor leadership: Characteristics and practices.* Manuscript submitted for publication

Young, A., Millard, T., & Miller-Kneale, M. (2013). Enhancing school counselor instructional leadership through collaborative teaming: Implications for principals. *National Association for Secondary School Principals* (In Press).

CHAPTER 4

Educational Models of Influence

"Effective leadership is not about making speeches or being liked; leadership is defined by results, not attributes."
Peter Drucker

There are times in our professional career and personal life that we think of leadership in the broad sense. We may think of many types of influences such as organizational, business and educational leadership. We may also think of frequently cited leadership styles such as authoritarian, democratic or laissez faire (Guastello, 1995; Lewin, Lippitt, & White, 1939; Northhouse, 2012). However, given the context of school counselor leaders as horizontal or vertical leaders and the characteristics of resourceful problem-solving, systemic collaboration, social justice advocacy, interpersonal influence and professional efficacy, discussed in chapter three, let's examine educational approaches that can influence and increase school counselors' capacity to lead.

Although there are many educational leadership models, in this chapter we examine three approaches to guide the process of increasing sustainability and ground the theoretical foundation for horizontal and vertical school counselor leadership. They may be used independently or collectively, depending on the situation or leader's identified characteristics. The first approach, the Four-Framework Approach, was developed by Bolman and Deal (1997; 2008). The second, 21 Responsibilities for School Leaders, by Marzano, Walter and McNulty (2005), focuses on instructional leadership responsibilities, which can also be critical for school counselors to shape optimal educational outcomes for students (Marzano, 2003; Marzano, 2010). The third approach, a Framework for Shared Leadership by Lambert (2002; 2003), examines the impact of shared influence on decision making.

FOUR-FRAMEWORK APPROACH

The ASCA National Model details the relationship of the Four-Framework Approach (structural, human resource, political and symbolic) for school counselor leaders and suggests circumstances may determine the approaches that are appropriate given the time and situation. The framework is highlighted within this chapter and in the ASCA National Model (2012, pp. 2-3). Additionally, Dollarhide (2003) examined the value of school counselors using the Four-Framework Approach.

Structural: The structural leader designs and implements a process or structure that is appropriate to a particular problem or circumstance to identify goals, delineate authoritarian boundaries and complete tasks. Structural leaders are able to recognize and articulate the consequences of tasks that are unaccomplished or goals that are not well-defined. An example of school counseling structural leadership may occur during the process of identifying school counseling program foci or goals and adhering to program competencies (ASCA, 2012). Structural leadership skills are also demonstrated during the data assessment process of analyzing formative and summative program assessments with the goal of continual program improvement.

Human resource: The human resource leader views people as the heart of the organization and attempts to be responsive to the needs of individuals to gain commitment and loyalty. Human resource leaders are active listeners who believe in their people, use empathic communication and stress member support and empowerment. This leader empowers people through engagement and securing resources needed to perform the job well. However, human resource leaders are willing to confront challenges when deemed necessary by using supportive techniques. This approach is appropriate when morale is low or declining but resources are relatively abundant. School counselor leaders exhibit human resource leadership within the context of the ASCA National Model when the leader articulates and publicizes the alignment of school counseling program goals to stakeholders. Publishing the school counseling calendar electronically in newsletters can be the conduit to share scheduled activities and programs.

Political: The political leader understands the political realities of the organization and can overcome challenges while sustaining stakeholder interest. This leader operates within the distribution of power and is often able to succeed with limited resources. Conflict is managed by grounding and building power bases with stakeholders. Political leaders initiate situations to negotiate differences, seek reasonable compromise and use their persuasiveness while finding commonalities among groups. The political leader is present and actively engages in schoolwide and districtwide decisions and brings together the necessary stakeholders to ensure success for all students. An example is actively advocating for equitable school counseling resources at school board meetings.

Symbolic: The symbolic leader is visible and views vision as critical because people respond when they believe in something. Symbolism becomes an important aspect when communicating the organization's mission. These leaders often rely on organizational traditions and values as a base for building a common vision and culture providing cohesiveness and meaning. School counselor leadership examples are presenting results data, initiating activities that promote student achievement and adhering to the ASCA Ethical Standards for School Counselors (ASCA, 2010).

Now, let's briefly summarize the Four-Framework Approach as it relates to school counselor leadership. Within the structural approach both horizontal and vertical leaders define program focus, select appropriate student competencies and adhere to professional development. Vertical leaders also identify professional development needs for school counselors. The horizontal and vertical human resource school counselor leader believes in people and communicates that belief through visibility and accessibility. The political school counselor leader builds linkages with stakeholders and is a negotiator. Finally, the symbolic leader uses symbols and metaphors to gain attention of followers. Most importantly, symbolic leaders lead by example.

Theory into Practice – Four-Framework Activity

The chart below provides examples of school counselor leadership characteristics and practices aligned with the Four-Framework Approach. Consider the previous discussion and the examples provided below to identify your own leadership practices and how they align with the Four-Framework Approach and the school counselor leadership characteristics presented in chapter three.

Figure 4.1

Four-Framework Approach	School Counseling Examples and Characteristics	Your Examples
Structural	Design strategies for growth of the school counseling program *Resourceful Problem-Solving* *Social Justice Advocacy*	
Human Resource	Visible and accessible *Systemic Collaboration* *Social Justice Advocacy*	
Political	Understand distribution of power *Interpersonal Influence* *Social Justice Advocacy*	
Symbolic	Lead by example *Professional Efficacy* *Social Justice Advocacy*	

21 RESPONSIBILITIES FOR SCHOOL LEADERS

In addition to having the knowledge and skills to implement school counseling practices, horizontal and vertical school counselor leaders should also understand and use instructional best practices. School counselors who understand and use instructional best practices develop a credible reputation, become an ally to teachers and the principal and are an indispensable educational resource (Young, Millard, & Miller-Kneale, 2013). School counselors who fail to integrate themselves within the instructional program run the risk of being viewed as a nonessential part of the education process. School counselor leaders must recognize the importance of making their programs an integral part of instruction and align with the principal's vision.

Marzano, Waters and McNulty's (2005) framework is based on meta-analyses and extensive research about instructional leadership, promoting student achievement promotion and effective leadership practices implementation. Combining knowledge and skills is the foundation of balanced leadership. Although there are 21 leadership responsibilities identified that correlate with student academic achievement, within the context of school counselor leadership, we focus on six of the responsibilities that more closely align with school counseling (Marzano, Waters, & McNulty, 2005, pp. 44-45).

1. Focus: establish clear goals and keep those goals in the forefront of the school's attention by communicating and operating from strong ideals and beliefs about education.
2. Outreach: advocate and serve as a spokesperson for the school to all stakeholders.
3. Situational awareness: aware of the details and undercurrent regarding the functioning of the school and use this information to address current and potential problems.
4. Involvement in curriculum, instruction and assessment: direct involvement in the design and implementation of curriculum, instruction and assessment practices.
5. Monitoring/evaluating: monitor the effectiveness of school practices and their impact on student learning.
6. Change agent: maintain a disposition to challenge the status quo.

For example, a horizontal school counselor leader may serve as a liaison between instructional departments and the school counseling department. The vertical school counselor leader might maintain collaborative relationships with state and/or national leaders. At both levels they use multiple data resources to improve student achievement and lead the process of developing goals, specifically SMART goals.

ACTIVITY: **Theory into Practice – 21 Responsibilities Activity**

The following chart provides examples of school counselor leadership characteristics and practices aligning with the 21 Responsibilities for School Leaders. Consider the previous discussion and the examples provided in the chart to identify your own leadership practices and how they align with the 21 Responsibilities for School Leaders and the school counselor leadership characteristics presented in chapter three.

Figure 4.2

21 Responsibilities for School Leaders	School Counseling Examples and Characteristics	Your Examples
Involvement in Curriculum, Instruction and Assessment	Serve as liaison between instructional and school counseling department *Systemic Collaboration*	
Situational Awareness	Write a grant to address a situation impeding student success *Resourceful Problem-Solving*	
Focus	Serve in a leadership role on the school improvement plan team *Interpersonal Influence*	
Outreach	Serve on state or national councils having an impact on school counseling *Systemic Collaboration*	
Monitoring and Evaluating	Share outcome data to advocate for additional staff to serve under-represented populations *Social Justice Advocacy*	
Change Agent	Lead the charge to challenge inequitable practices *Professional Efficacy* *Social Justice Advocacy*	

FRAMEWORK FOR SHARED LEADERSHIP

The third approach is proposed by Linda Lambert (2002) and presents theoretical concepts of shared leadership capacity through a constructivist lens. The assumptions are applicable to the role and expectations of school counselors aspiring to acquire leadership skills and demonstrate related practices when working in preK-12 school settings (Lambert, 2003). Viewing leadership as action-oriented allows educators to focus on processes, activities and relationships, rather than accomplish specific tasks (Lambert, 1998). Lambert, Walker, Zimmerman, Cooper, Lambert, Gardner and Szabo (2002) refer to this process as "constructivist leadership," which relates to educators who construct meanings toward a shared purpose.

The concept of constructivist leadership is based on the same ideals that underlie constructivist learning: the process of acquiring meaning and knowledge, seeking inquiry, participating activly and engaging in self-reflection (Lambert et al., 2002). The primary function of leadership becomes the engagement of people in processes that create conditions to form common ground about learning. For school counselor horizontal and vertical leaders this means increasing leadership capacity to create a school counseling environment promoting academic achievement and personal growth. Increased leadership capacity means: (a) principals, school counselors, teachers and parents are mutual learners and leaders (Young, 2004), (b) student motivation and achievement are high or steadily improving (Marzano, 2010), and (c) reflective practices enable participants to consider and reconsider ways to perform tasks better that lead to improved results (Mason & McMahon, 2009). Thus, the constructivist view of shared leadership capacity can be applicable to school counselor leaders, as well as principals and teachers.

Lambert (1998, 2002) identifies five key assumptions that create a conceptual framework to enhance leadership capacity. Each assumption equates to what is currently known or needed within the school counseling profession. The first assumption suggests that "leadership" and "leader" imply different meanings. The focus is not solely on the leader's "acts or traits," and leadership can be demonstrated in a broader sense. Lambert (2002) suggests, "Leadership is broader than the sum total of its leaders for it also involves an energy flow or synergy generated by those who choose to lead" (p. 5). Thus, school counselor leaders comprehending this assumption construct and negotiate meaning to bring about change for students. This assumption was evident in the resourceful problem-solving factor of the school counselor leadership survey.

The second assuming factor connects leadership to learning that eventually leads to constructive change. By understanding the connection between learning and leading, individuals begin to assume responsibility for the learning of individuals other than students. Consequently, learning becomes a reciprocal process through the collaboration of committed stakeholders. For horizontal and vertical leaders this means the collaborative commitment to create a community of learners and foster a climate of high expectations.

Third, everyone has the potential to serve as a leader. If such is the case, school counselors can learn how to develop and lead learning environments by constructing meaning from their own experiences and by bringing new knowledge, skills and theories into practice.

This assumption reinforces the influence of graduate preparation and continuous professional development training in the school counseling profession. For instance, graduate field experiences (practicum and internship) and first-year school counselors can create a foundation for knowledge gained and beliefs formed.

The fourth assumption contends leading is a shared endeavor and the foundation for the democratization of schools. This assumption becomes a challenge for horizontal school counselor leaders who may work as the only school counselor in their building. Therefore, it is important they form a network consortium to share ideas and receive feedback. Accomplishing goals is a collective endeavor, and individuals are most effective in demonstrating leadership skills in the presence of others so feedback, self-reflection and evaluation become continuous (Lambert et al., 2002).

Finally, leadership requires the redistribution of power and authority. Lambert (2002) proposed principals should release authority and learn how to enhance power and informal authority. Shared learning, purpose and the responsibility demand the reciprocal realignment of power and authority for school counselor leaders at all levels.

Theory into Practice – Framework for Shared Leadership

The chart below provides examples of school counselor leadership characteristics and practices aligned with the Framework for Shared Leadership. Consider the previous discussion and the examples provided below to identify your own leadership practices and how they align with the Framework for Shared Leadership and the school counselor leadership characteristics presented in chapter three.

Figure 4.3

Framework for Shared Leadership	School Counselor Leadership Characteristic	Your Example
Assumption 1: Leadership is broad.	Co-chair a schoolwide or districtwide endeavor. *Resource Problem-Solving*	
Assumption 2: Leadership is connected to learning.	Plan and facilitate workshops to stakeholders articulating the alignment of best instructional school practices to close achievement and opportunity gaps. *Social Justice Advocacy*	
Assumption 3: Everyone has potential to lead.	Accept the responsibility to lead a school counseling program. *Professional Efficacy*	
Assumption 4: Leadership is a shared endeavor.	Plan and develop a school counseling collaborative district team process. *Systemic Collaboration*	
Assumption 5: Power and authority are redistributed.	Transition from horizontal to vertical leadership responsibilities. *Interpersonal Influence*	

REFERENCES

American School Counselor Association (2012). *The ASCA National Model: A framework for school counseling programs* (3rd. ed.). Alexandria, VA: Author.

American School Counselor Association (2010). *Ethical standards for school counselors.* Alexandria, VA: Author.

Bolman, L. G., & Deal, T. E. (1997). *Reframing organizations: Artisty, choice and leadership* (4th ed.). San Francisco: Jossey-Bass.

Bolman, L. G., & Deal, T. E. (2008). *Reframing organizations: Artisty, choice and leadership* (4th ed.). San Francisco: Jossey-Bass.

Dollarhide, C. T. (2003). School counselors as program leaders: Applying leadership contexts to school counseling. *Professional School Counseling, 6,* 304-308.

Guastello, S. J. (1995). Facilitative style, individual innovation, and emergent leadership in problem-solving groups. *The Journal of Creative Behavior, 29,* 4, 225-239.

Lambert, L. (1998). *Building leadership capacity in schools.* Alexandria, ASCD.

Lambert, L. (2002). A framework for shared leadership. *Educational Leadership, 58,* 8, 37-40.

Lambert, L. (2003). *Leadership capacity for lasting school improvement.* Alexandria, VA: Association for Supervision and Curriculum Development.

Lambert, L., Walker, D., Zimmerman, D., Cooper, J., Lambert, M. D., Gardner, M., Szabo, D. (2002) *The constructivist leader.* (2 ed.) New York: Teachers College Press.

Lewin, K. L., Lippitt, R., & White, R. K. (1939). Patterns of aggressive behaviors in experimentally created social climates. *Journal of Social Psychology, 10,* 271-290.

Marzano, R. (2003). *What works in schools: Translating research into action.* Alexandria, VA: Association for Supervision and Curriculum Development.

Marzano, R. (2010). High expectations for all. *Educational Leadership, 68,* 82-85.

Marzano, R., Waters, T., & McNulty, B. (2005). *School leadership that works: From research to results.* Alexandria, VA: Association for Supervision and Curriculum Development.

Mason E., & McMahon, G. (2009). Leadership practices. *Professional School Counseling 13,* 2, 106.

Northhouse, P. (2012). *Introduction to leadership: Concepts and practice.* Thousand Oaks, CA: Sage.

Young, A. (2004). *Preparing school counselor leaders: The perceptions and practices of transforming school counseling initiative graduates from The Ohio State University.* (Unpublished doctoral dissertation). The Ohio State University, Columbus, OH.

Young, A., Millard, T., & Miller-Kneale, M. (2013). Enhancing school counselor instructional leadership through collaborative teaming: Implications for principals. *National Association for Secondary School Principals* (In Press).

CHAPTER 5

Accountable Leaders

"Having the data isn't enough. It is essential to use the data to drive student achievement."
Arne Duncan

In this chapter we discuss the importance of using a process to infuse data as a school counselor leader. When school counselor leaders articulate how students are different as a result of the school counseling program, they are positioned to lead the conversation around what the educational outcomes should be for students (Hines & Lemon, 2011). Although No Child Left Behind (2002) increased the focus on mastery of content knowledge through standardized assessments, the current educational and employment landscape surrounding Race to the Top (2009) has created a heightened awareness around issues of college and career readiness. Thus, the conversation has broadened around what students should know and be able to do as a result of K-12 education (Isaacs, 2003). School counselor leaders understand that closing achievement and opportunity gaps is a critical piece of this work that must be undertaken by an entire school or system; however, schools must go beyond traditional measures of performance if all students will graduate college- and career-ready.

In a survey conducted by the National Office for School Counselor Advocacy (NOSCA), True North: Charting the Course to College and Career Readiness, the findings suggest school counselors with no system of accountability work at schools with the lowest rates of college-going students (NOSCA, 2012). Further, they identified a correlation between certain types of school counselor accountability and higher college attendance rates, even after controlling for other factors such as caseload, years of experience and school counselor education level. It is clear school counselor accountability is critical to moving forward the national agenda of college and career readiness, and both horizontal and vertical school counselor leaders can use accountability measures to support schools and districts in informed decision-making promoting equitable outcomes for all students.

GETTING STARTED WITH DATA

School counselors must use data at each phase of program delivery and assessment to make decisions (Dimmitt, Carey, & Hatch, 2007; Kaffenberger, 2012). This means quantitative and qualitative data are collected and analyzed when establishing school counseling goals, assessing the effectiveness of programs and interventions and advocating for necessary changes to improve student outcomes (Fraenkel, Whallen, & Hyun, 2011; Kaffenberger & Young, 2013). School counselors may find it difficult to determine where to start if they are not familiar with using accountability measures to drive their programs. The data cycle for school counseling programs (Figure 5.1) provides horizontal and vertical school counselor leaders with a process for data collection and analysis they can use to inform programs and improve student outcomes.

Data Cycle for School Counseling Programs (Figure 5.1)

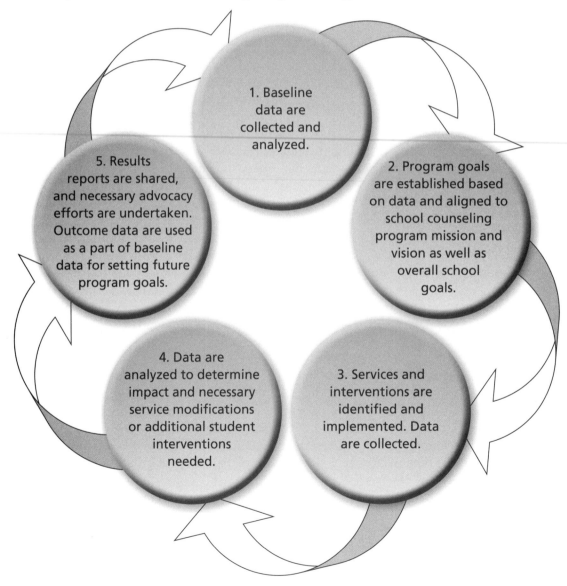

UNDERSTANDING THE DATA CYCLE

School counselor leaders must begin with identifying where students are prior to determining goals, programs and interventions. Establishing baseline data will also allow school counselor leaders to determine program and intervention impact. The school and district goals serve as guides to identify what data to collect (ASCA, 2012; Kaffenberger & Young, 2013). As baseline, perception and student outcome data are collected, disaggregated and analyzed, school counselor leaders are able to identify gaps existing between student groups and better understand the underlying causes of achievement, behavior and attendance issues to set program goals and plan interventions accordingly (Haycock, 2001; Rowell, 2006; Stone & Dahir, 2011). The School Counseling Survey Considerations Template serve as a guide to identify who, what, why and how to collect perception data. It is designed to guide school counselor leaders in the collection and analysis of needs assessment or survey data.

Figure 5.2 School Counseling Survey Considerations Template

What information do we hope to gain by distributing this survey?			
How do we plan to use the information gained from the survey? (Check all that apply.) ___ To develop school counseling program goals/interventions based on student needs ___To assess impact of current services/programs ___ To advocate for services or programs supporting students ___ Other (Please explain.)			
Given our survey goals, which stakeholders will we need to survey? (Check all that apply.) ___ Parents ___ Students ___ Staff ___Other (Please explain.)			
Given our goals, will we survey all stakeholders in the identified population or a representative sample (e.g.: ninth-grade parents and students, retained students, students with one or more failing grades) to get the information we need? ___ All stakeholders in the identified group ___Representative sample ___Targeted group (Identify group.)			
Is the purpose of this survey aligned to our school counseling vision and mission? (Circle your answer. If not aligned, note comments below.)	Strongly Aligned	Somewhat Aligned	Not Aligned
Are the results of the survey likely to provide meaningful data we can use to have an impact on student performance, behavior or engagement? (Circle your answer. If unlikely, note comments below.)	Highly Likely	Somewhat Likely	Unlikely
What is the likelihood we can use the survey results within the next six months?	Highly Likely	Somewhat Likely	Unlikely

Survey Content Review

	Yes	No
Will the format and delivery method of the survey allow for easy data analysis? Comments:	Yes	No
Is the purpose of the survey clear to stakeholders, and are confidentiality issues addressed? Comments:	Yes	No
If the results of the survey will be disaggregated, is there a request for appropriate demographic information included on the survey? Comments:	Yes	No
Is the length of the survey appropriate to the audience? Comments:	Yes	No
Are the questions easy-to-understand, user-friendly and developmentally appropriate to the targeted audience? Comments:	Yes	No
Do any of the questions ask for information already available through other sources? Comments:	Yes	No
Are the questions aligned to student competencies? Comments:	Yes	No
Additional Comments:		

Once goals are set, school counselor leaders should plan services and interventions to determine how to achieve the goals. Services and interventions may occur at multiple levels including individual, group, classroom, grade-level, schoolwide or districtwide interventions. In some cases, school counselor leaders will directly deliver the services and support; in other cases, they will collaborate with other educational stakeholders and use the data to influence needed changes (Haycock, 2001; Holcomb-McCoy, 2007). As programs and interventions are delivered, data are collected. School counselor leaders then analyze the results, determine program impact and implications and identify modifications or additional student interventions needed. Finally, they share results reports to inform stakeholders and advocate for necessary changes to programs or services. The data from the results report become a part of the baseline data for establishing future goals. To see how the data cycle looks when applied to the issue of students with failing grades, review the following case study.

CASE STUDY

Failing Grades and the Data Cycle for School Counseling Programs

Merit Middle School has a problem; 50 percent of its students received at least one failing grade in the previous school year. The principal is incredibly concerned about this statistic as the school mission is to ensure all students reach their academic potential. As a part of school planning, the school team identifies a goal of reducing the total percentage of students receiving a failing grade by 25 percent. The school counselors at Merit Middle School understand the importance of aligning their program goals with the overall school goals and being able to identify what baseline data they need to determine how to best achieve this goal.

The school counselors meet as a collaborative learning team and agree to collect and analyze the following to better understand the failing grades:

- Failure data disaggregated by grade level, subject, teacher and No Child Left Behind subgroups
- Teacher survey data to identify their perceptions around why students are failing courses
- Attendance data for students failing courses
- Discipline data for students failing courses
- Data on existing intervention efforts
- Survey data from students with failing grades

After reviewing the data, the school counselors determine students are failing more frequently in seventh grade (their first year in middle school), and teachers report a lack of foundational academic habits is causing many students to fail. Finally, only 35 percent of seventh-grade students report they are comfortable asking school staff for help. As a result the school counselors set a SMART goal to reduce the percentage of seventh-grade students with an end-of-year failing grade by 25 percent as compared with the previous school year.

School counselors collaborate with administrators and seventh-grade teachers and implement the following programs and interventions to address this goal:

- Each seventh-grade subject area will be assigned a specific day of the week that they can assign homework (math Monday, science Tuesday, English Wednesday, history Thursday and electives Friday)
- School counselors will deliver lessons on study skills, time management, organization, stress management and self-advocacy through homeroom during the first nine weeks of school.
- Students with failing grades at the end of the first quarter who are not effectively using good academic habits will be identified for participation in school counseling small groups during the second quarter.
- School counselors and teachers from the seventh-grade team will develop and deliver parent education seminars as well as seventh-grade newsletters to provide parents and guardians with information to support their child's academic success.

At the end of the second quarter, school counselors analyze data from the classroom lessons, small groups and parent programs and identify that failing grades are declining for all subgroups except for students with chronic attendance problems. The school counselors identify additional interventions for this group, including biweekly individual goal-setting meetings, assignment of a staff mentor and referrals to the attendance officer and school social worker.

At the end of the school year, the school counselors prepare results reports to share with their principal, the seventh-grade teachers, the school counseling advisory council and other stakeholders. They see a 20 percent decrease in the percentage of seventh-grade students with failing grades; however, students with chronic attendance issues are still receiving a high rate of failing grades. The school counselors advocate making attendance a schoolwide goal for the following year, and the principal and the school planning team agree.

PROCESS, PERCEPTION AND OUTCOME DATA

School counselors must collect process, perception and outcome data to show who is being served by the program, what stakeholders believe they can do as a result of programs or interventions and how programs and interventions ultimately affect student achievement, attendance and behavior (ASCA, 2012). Likewise, school counselor horizontal and vertical leaders comprehend the importance of using and articulating all aspects of process, perception and outcome data. Process data provide evidence an event occurred, demonstrate how many participants were involved and account for the duration of the program or intervention (ASCA, 2012). Process data support school counselor leaders' understanding of who is being reached through their delivery and who is not being served. Process data help identify if programs need to be refined or abandoned when considered together with outcome data. For example, if a summer ninth-grade transition program does not result in decreased retention rates and increased student participation in courses of rigor, should the program be eliminated, or should other factors be considered such as number of sessions or program content? While process data are most useful to school counselors in the delivery of services, it does not always speak to the impact the services have on students.

Perception data help school counselor leaders understand what stakeholders think they know, believe or can do and are collected through self-reports. School counselors obtain perception data through pre-post tests, needs assessments, program evaluations and exit surveys (ASCA, 2012). Perception data support school counselors in understanding how stakeholders believe they are affected by the program; however, unless it is linked to outcome data, the question still remains: so what? Outcome data answer that question by linking school counseling program impact to improvements in achievement, attendance and behavior (ASCA, 2012).

Outcome data are collected from multiple sources and depending on each school or district outcome data may or may not be easily accessible. For example, response to intervention (RTI) programs support school counselors in linking their interventions to outcome data. School counselor leaders in schools with or without RTI can advocate for data systems allowing them to better monitor student progress and the impact of interventions provided to struggling students. To do this, school counselor leaders need to communicate what data should be monitored to ensure positive outcomes for all students based on factors linked to student success.

Process, Perception and Outcome Data Activity

Use this activity to review samples of data to check your understanding between the different types of data school counselors collect and analyze. Review each of the statements below. Identify if the statement represents (a) process, (b) perception or (c) outcome data.

Figure 5.3

1. Forty-five students participated in the essay-writing workshop. _____

2. Eighth-grade retention rates were reduced by 10 percent. _____

3. Eighty-five percent of the students who participated in the honors boot camp passed at least one honors course. _____

4. Seventy-five percent of the fourth-grade students know how to report bullying. _____

5. Two hundred parents participated in the parent education workshop. _____

6. Sixteen percent of sixth-grade students feel unsafe on the bus. _____

7. Sixty-eight percent of juniors took the SAT or ACT. _____

8. Ninety-two percent of the students who participated in the study skills group improved their grades. _____

Answers: 1. a, 2. c, 3. c, 4. b, 5. a, 6. b, 7. a, 8. c

DATA ANALYSIS AND MONITORING

Under the current education accountability system, No Child Left Behind Act (NCLB) of 2001, a school's measure of effectiveness is based on students meeting proficiency objectives in reading and math, participation rates in state assessments, and graduation and attendance rates. In 2013, 37 states and the District of Columbia received waivers from the U.S. Department of Education from NCLB in exchange for rigorous and comprehensive state-

level plans designed to improve educational outcomes for all students, close achievement gaps, increase equity and improve the quality of instruction (DOE, 2013). As local school districts align to state expectations and individual schools align to district expectations, it should be of no surprise to school counselor leaders that accountability measures for school counselors must align to these rigorous expectations as well (Young & Kaffenberger, 2011).

School counselor leaders must determine what types of data should be reviewed, analyzed and tracked each year to inform the school counseling program and how data will be disaggregated to increase college and career readiness. The National High School Center Report (2007) linked high school completion with factors beginning in elementary school. Specifically, poor grades in core academic subjects, low attendance rates, grade-level retention and disengagement in the classroom serve as better predictors of dropout than student background factors (Kennelly & Riechl, 2007). Horizontal and vertical school counselor leaders, however, must pay attention to correlations between gender, socioeconomic status, ethnicity and high school graduation when developing culturally responsive programs. The type of data tracked will depend greatly on the needs and goals of the school or district, the availability of data and the students' grade level. The following data-monitoring activity provides horizontal and vertical leaders with data points to consider based on the school's needs and goals.

ACTIVITY: Data-Monitoring Activity

Review the following examples of process, perception and outcome data based on your current leadership (horizontal or vertical). Vertical leaders should consider their role in responding to both sets of data. Next to each example, identify if you are currently collecting and analyzing these data (Y), need to consider collecting and analyzing these data in the future (F) or do not see the data example as something appropriate to your school counseling program (N/A). Once you have responded to each of the data elements, answer the reflection questions.

Figure 5.4 Examples of Process, Perception, and Outcome Data

Process Data for Horizontal Leaders

___ Participation in school counseling programs or interventions
___ Participation in extracurricular and enrichment activities
___ Enrollment in courses of rigor or remedial courses
___ Free Application for Federal Student Aid (FAFSA) completion rates
___ Participation in college entrance exams (PSAT, SAT, ACT, TOEFL)

Perception Data for Horizontal Leaders

___ College and career awareness and aspirations
___ Self-advocacy behaviors
___ 21st-century skills (ex: collaboration, communication)
___ Ownership of learning (ex: goal setting)
___ Self-regulation behaviors (ex: can delay gratification)
___ Persistence and motivation
___ Academic and learning strategies (ex: study skills)
___ Needs assessment data
___ Students feeling safe at school

Outcome Data for Horizontal Leaders

___ Retention rates
___ Graduation rates
___ Completion of advanced academic coursework
___ Diploma types earned
___ Scores on college entrance exams
___ Course failure rates
___ Reading on grade-level
___ Scores on state assessments
___ Suspension and expulsion rates
___ Attendance rates
___ College enrollment rates
___ Completion of college-level coursework (AP, IB, dual-enrollment)

Process Data for Vertical Leaders

___ School counselor attrition rates
___ Number of times technology resources were accessed
___ Percentage of school counselor time spent in non-school-counseling-related activities
___ School counselor participation in professional development offerings
___ School counselor caseloads

Perception Data for Vertical Leaders

___ School counselor professional development needs
___ Pre and post assessments from school counselor professional development activities
___ School counselors' perceptions of self-efficacy and leadership skills
___ School counselor belief of ability to implement comprehensive school counseling programs

Outcome Data for Vertical Leaders

___ Retention of school counselors in high-needs schools
___ Hiring of diverse population of school counselors as a result of recruitment efforts

Reminder: Vertical school counselor leaders are also accountable for horizontal outcome data.

Data Monitoring Activity Reflective Questions:

1. For each of the data points you marked "Y," are you disaggregating the data so you can better understand what the data mean for the school or district and for subgroups?

2. If you marked items as "F" for future consideration, how might those data point support your work in a school or district?

3. If you marked items as N/A, would it be useful to know that information from your feeder schools (elementary, middle or high) who may be collecting and analyzing those data?

REFERENCES

American School Counselor Association (2012). *The ASCA National Model: A framework for school counseling programs* (3rd ed.). Alexandria, VA: Author.

Dimmitt, C., Carey, J., & Hatch, T. (2007). *Evidence-based school counseling: Making a difference with data-driven practices.* Thousand Oaks, CA: Corwin Press.

Fraenkel, J., Wallen, N., & Hyun, H. (2011). *How to design & evaluate research in education.* (8th ed.) Boston, MA: McGraw Hill.

Haycock, K. (2001). Closing the achievement gap. *Educational Leadership, 58,* 6-11.

Hines, P., & Lemon, R. (2011). *Poised to Lead: How School Counselors Can Drive College and Career Readiness.* http://www.edtrust.org/dc/publication/poised-to-lead. Retrieved on February 16, 2013.

Holcomb-McCoy, C. (2007). *School counseling to close the achievement gap: A social justice framework for success.* Thousand Oaks, CA: Corwin Press

Isaacs, M. L. (2003). Data-driven decision making: The engine of accountability. *Professional School Counseling, 6,* 288-295.

Kaffenberger, C. (2012). What does it mean to have a data-driven school counseling program? In *ASCA National Model: A framework for school counseling programs* (3rd ed.; pp. 117-119). Alexandria, VA: American School Counselor Association.

Kaffenberger, C., & Young, A. (2013). *Making DATA Work* (3rd ed.). Alexandria, VA: American School Counselor Association.

Kennelly, L. & Riechl, C. (2007). *Approaches to dropout prevention: Heeding early warning signs interventions.* National High School Center.

National Office for School Counselor Advocacy (2012). http://media.collegeboard.com/digitalServices/pdf/nosca/true-north.pdf. Retrieved on January 25, 2013.

Race to the Top. http://www2.ed.gov/programs/racetothetop/index.html. Retrieved on March 1, 2013.

Rowell, L. L. (2006). Action research and school counseling: Closing the gap between research and practice. *Professional School Counseling, 9,* 376-384.

Stone, C. B., & Dahir, C. A. (2011) *School counselor accountability: A MEASURE of student success* (3rd ed.). Upper Saddle River, NJ: Merrill/Prentice.

United States Department of Education (2002). The no child left behind act of 2001. Retrieved from http://www.ed.gov/policy/elsec/leg/esea02/107-110.pdf.

United States Department of Education (2013). Obama administration approves three more NCLB flexibility requests – 37 states and DC now approved for waivers. http://www.ed.gov/news/press-releases/obama-administration-approves-three-more-nclb-flexibility-requests37-states. Retrieved May 29, 2013.

Young, A. & Kaffenberger, C. (2011). The beliefs and practices of school counselors who use data to implement comprehensive school counseling programs. *Professional School Counseling, 15,* 67-76.

CHAPTER 6

Leading for Equity

"Injustice anywhere is a threat to justice everywhere."
Martin Luther King Jr.

School counselor leaders must seek socially just outcomes for students. Although high school dropout rates appear to be on a decline throughout the United States, blacks, Hispanics, American Indians and Alaska Natives are still dropping out at much higher rates as compared with their white and Asian peers. Additionally, students attending high-poverty schools are less likely to graduate as compared with students attending low-poverty schools (*http://nces.ed.gov/programs/coe/analysis/2010-section3b.asp*). Racial, gender, ability and language inequities also exist when considering student discipline rates that may compound the dropout problem. The gaps that exist for high school completion are mirrored in college completion rates, with females completing college at higher rates than males and white and Asian students completing college at higher rates than black and Hispanic students *http://nces.ed.gov/programs/coe/indicator_pgr.asp*.

The inequity patterns existing for students in preK-12 must be addressed to ensure students are not disproportionately at risk for unemployment, incarceration, poverty or other social and economic challenges they may face as a result of an inequitable education. In this chapter, we examine the role of the school counselor leader in shaping policies and practices resulting in equitable outcomes for students.

Cross, Bazron, Dennis and Isaacs' (1989) work on cultural competence provides early foundations for approaching cross-cultural helping relationships. They refer to cultural competence as a set of congruent behaviors, attitudes and policies that come together in a system, agency or among professionals enabling them to work effectively in cross-cultural situations (Cross et al., 1989). Several researchers (Holcomb-McCoy, 2005; Holcomb-McCoy & Myers, 1999; Lindsey, Roberts, & CampbellJones, 2005; Reeves, 2008; Stephens, Lindsey, & Randall, 2011; Terrell & Lindsey, 2008) have expanded the field including developing a continuum where practices can be measured. For example, Holcomb-McCoy (2005) broached the topic of cultural proficiency by investigating the multicultural perception of school counselors using a modified version of the Multicultural Counseling Competence and Training Survey (MCCTS) based on the Association of Multicultural Counseling and Development (AMCD) Multicultural Competencies and Explanatory Statements (Arredondo, Toporek, Brown, Jones, Locke, Sanchez, & Stadler, 1996). A contrasting difference between cultural competence and cultural proficiency necessitates moving beyond personal and professional practices that model culturally appropriate behaviors to advocating for a system that effectively serves the educational needs of all groups to ensure a socially just society (Lindsey, Robins, & Terrell, 2009). Cultural proficiency is, therefore, an essential component for school counselor horizontal and vertical leaders engaged in social justice work addressing inequities, removing barriers and empowering students and families in the process.

SCHOOLS AND SYSTEMS

An educator's inability to effectively recognize and address cultural insensitivity or systems and procedures influencing and affecting students from different backgrounds in disproportionate ways leads to widening achievement and opportunity gaps resulting in inequitable outcomes for students and limited economic opportunities for postsecondary graduates (College Board, 2007). School counselor leaders must recognize and address the policies and practices (cultural bias, insensitivities, etc.) that continue to disadvantage certain groups of students while advantaging others by developing awareness within the school counseling program, providing professional development to colleagues to inform educational practices and advocating for culturally appropriate practices to ensure traditionally marginalized students are served by the education system (Grothaus, 2012; Terrell & Lindsey, 2008; Singleton & Linton, 2006). School counselor leaders must help "bring to light" factors affecting student achievement both within and outside of the school and identify strategic partnerships to address these factors or mitigate the impact on the student (Bryan & Henry, 2011).

Schools and school systems that do not examine the impact of policies and practices on student outcomes may continue to face achievement gaps and inequitable outcomes for students Grothaus (2012). A careful examination of hiring practices, training and evaluation of employees, instructional strategies and content, parent and community communication and outreach, and district regulations can reveal how culturally proficient an organization is and what changes need to be made to promote equity. School counselor leaders must call attention to those policies and practices that disadvantage certain groups of students and use outcome data to advocate for change. By addressing the inequitable policies, procedures or instructional conditions that may impede students' academic achievement, college access, career readiness or personal/social development, school counselors serve as advocates for socially just outcomes (Hatch, 2012 p. 14).

ACTIVITY: Culturally Competent Policies and Practices Activity

Use the following School Counselor Leadership Equity Profile to identify equitable policies and practices within your school or district. First, list the total number of students who are in each of the groups listed across the top of the chart. Next, fill in the percent of students in each group who meet the criteria. Finally, use the data from the profile to answer the Culturally Competent Policies and Practices reflective questions to identify changes your current school or district may need to address to promote achievement for all students. Note: The ASCA National Model school data profile template (ASCA, 2012) also provides a starting point for reviewing school data.

Figure 6.1 School Counselor Leader Equity Profile

Name: Date:

	All Students	Free/ Reduced Meals	English- Language Learners	Students with Disabilities	Black Students	Hispanic Students	Males	Females	Other Subgroups
Total Number of Students									
Enrolled in rigorous coursework									
Suspended or expelled									
Failed state assessments									
Retained in a grade level									
Attendance issues									
Participate in extracurricular activities									
Enrollment in alternative settings									

	All Students	Free/ Reduced Meals	English-Language Learners	Students with Disabilities	Black Students	Hispanic Students	Males	Females	Other Subgroups
Postsecondary two- or four-year college aspirations or plans									
Completed college readiness assessments – PSAT, SAT, ACT (secondary)									
On-time graduation (secondary)									
Earn industry licensure or certification (secondary)									

Reflective Questions: Equitable Policies and Practices

How do the current policies or practices in your school or district promote or limit student access to a full range of courses including courses of rigor that are necessary for college and career readiness?

How do you know when a student or family's cultural background and norms are misaligned with a school's policies? What would you do if this happened?

How do current policies and practices around discipline and attendance affect different student groups?

How do current policies or practices promote or limit student access to activities or enrichment opportunities?

How do current policies or practices promote or limit parental participation or partnership in the education process?

Do the educators in your school or district have the awareness, skills and knowledge necessary to engage in culturally proficient work leading to equitable outcomes? If not, what can be put in place to ensure they do?

CULTURAL PROFICIENCY STANDARDS

School counselors are provided with a framework of ethical and professional competencies addressing knowledge, skills, attitudes and beliefs they must have to work effectively in cross-cultural situations. For example:

- The American School Counselor Association (ASCA, 2012) embeds cultural proficiency expectations within the ASCA School Counselor Competencies and specifically addresses multicultural and social justice advocacy and leadership skills within the ASCA Ethical Standards for School Counselors (ASCA, 2010).
- The Association for Multicultural Counseling and Development (AMCD) identifies competencies that define the attitudes and beliefs, knowledge and skills necessary to engage in multicultural counseling as culturally skilled counselors. The competencies are grouped to address counselor self-awareness of cultural values and bias, counselor awareness of client's world view and culturally appropriate intervention strategies (Arredondo et al., 1996).
- The National Association of College Admission Counseling's (NACAC) Statement on Counselor Competencies (2000) addresses a school counselor's "ability to recognize, appreciate and serve cultural differences and the special needs of students and families" by identifying competencies for school counselors.

To illustrate the commonalities between ASCA, AMCD and NACAC competences, six themes are provided for consideration. They are: (a) reflective self-awareness, (b) knowledge, (c) skills, (d) practices, (e) advocacy and (f) responsiveness to deficits.

At the foundation of culturally proficient school counselor leadership is reflective self-awareness. There is a relationship between reflective practices and effective school leadership (Lindsey et al., 2009). School counselor horizontal and vertical leaders must explore their own race and culture and develop an understanding of how that intersects with the families and staff with whom they work. School counselor leaders must work to understand their strengths and weaknesses when it comes to multicultural work and actively seek to enhance their knowledge and skills to be able to engage in culturally proficient school counseling practices and advocacy work (Holcomb-McCoy & Chen-Haynes, 2011). Completing the reflective activities presented in this chapter will allow you to identify your own knowledge, skills, practices, advocacy and deficits and to use that information at the end of this chapter to complete a professional development plan to address how you will grow.

ACTIVITY: Cultural Proficiency Self-Reflection Activities

Three opportunities are provided in this chapter for you to reflect on the relationship between your cultural competency and leadership beliefs. First, complete the following cultural proficiency self-reflection activity based on the cited sample competencies from ASCA, AMCD and NACAC to rate yourself. Next, complete the Multicultural Counseling and Training Survey–Revised (MCCTS-R) developed by Holcomb-McCoy (2005) and score your results (Appendix A). Finally, respond to the reflective questions that follow the self-relfection activity.

Figure 6.2 Cultural Proficiency Self-Reflection Activity

	Not Like me	Somewhat Like Me	A lot Like Me	Always Like Me
I ensure my personal beliefs or values are not imposed on students or other stakeholders (ASCA, 2010).				
I recognize sources of discomfort with differences that exist between my students and me in terms of race, ethnicity and culture (AMCD,1996).				
I am aware of the stereotypes and preconceived notions I may hold toward other racial and ethnic minority groups (AMCD, 1996).				
I am able to recognize the limits of my multicultural competency and expertise (AMCD, 1996).				
I use inclusive and culturally responsive language in all forms of communication (ASCA, 2010).				
I acquaint students with the school-based and outreach services and support systems designed to address their unique educational needs (NACAC, 2000).				
I seek to improve and extend services to underserved students, especially those who are underrepresented among postsecondary education constituencies (NACAC, 2000).				
I work as an advocate and leader in my school or system to create equity-based school counseling programs that help close any achievement, opportunity and attainment gaps denying all students the chance to pursue their educational goals (ASCA, 2010).				
I acquire educational, consultation and training experiences to improve my awareness, knowledge, skills and effectiveness in working with diverse populations (ASCA, 2010).				

Reflective Questions

What do you believe are your current strengths as a culturally proficient school counselor leader?

What areas do you need to address to ensure your work with and on behalf of students is culturally responsive?

LEADERSHIP DILEMMAS

School counselor leaders face a variety of leadership dilemmas each day. It is critical to leaders' success to anticipate how they may respond to situations of cultural destructiveness, incapacity or blindness in advance of being confronted. Using the following culturally proficient responses to school scenarios, you can begin to understand where you may need to obtain additional skills and knowledge to respond to these situations in a culturally proficient manner. After answering the questions, discuss your responses with colleagues who have diverse views and perspectives to identify the similarities and differences in your responses.

ACTIVITY: **Culturally Proficient Responses to School Scenarios Activity**

Read each of scenarios that school counselor leaders may encounter in their work. Determine what the underlying assumptions may be; the skills and knowledge you may need to address the situation; and how personal beliefs, values and culture may affect your response. Then provide solutions.

Scenario 1: Student A is a rising fourth-grader who has qualified for gifted and talented (GT) services. The GT program in your school is a pull-out model where students are sent to a separate school for all of their courses. After visiting the GT program and attending the new student information session, Student A's parents are concerned that she will be the only African-American student there and that the faculty is not diverse. Although her parents feel she is bored in her current courses, they are concerned about sending her to the GT program and even more concerned that no other minority children were identified for the program. They request a meeting with you to address their concerns. What are your recommendations?

Scenario 2: Student B is a new 12th-grade student who transferred to your school from out of state. Her academic records indicate she was an outstanding student who had perfect attendance for the past three years. Two weeks after enrolling, she starts coming to school late, and her teachers are concerned as she is not doing any work at home. When you meet with Student B, she begins to cry as she tells you her father was deported prior to their move because he is undocumented, and she and her mother moved in with cousins because they were afraid the same thing would happen to them. The cousins have now threatened to contact immigration services if her mother does not pay more rent, requiring Student B to work late hours with her mother to ensure they have enough money. She is exhausted when she gets home, which has lead to her sleeping in and coming to school late. She asks you if it is possible to just get a GED because she thinks she can't to go to college anyway since she's undocumented. How do you respond to this situation?

Scenario 3: Student C is a rising seventh-grade student who is genetically male but has been dressing and identifying as a female since fifth grade. Her parents contact you over the summer to discuss her transition and participation in middle school programs. They are most concerned with the annual overnight seventh-grade trip, her physical education course and her desire to participate on the girl's club soccer team. They wish to discuss how the school will support her participation in these activities. You schedule a meeting with her parents, the seventh-grade teachers and administrator prior to school starting so you can discuss their concerns. Although all of the teachers are supportive during the meeting, after the meeting the seventh-grade administrator approaches you and expresses concerns. He suggests that perhaps you should be working with Student C on more appropriate expressions of her identity and discouraging her from "cross dressing." He is worried she is going to become a target of bullying and doesn't believe the school is safe for her given what he saw a few years ago with a similar situation. How would you proceed?

Scenario 4: Student D is a rising 10th-grade student who has done well academically and has recently been identified by his teachers for a college-readiness program targeting students who would be first-generation college students or face significant barriers to enrolling in college. His parents, both professionals and graduates of U.S. universities, contact you when they receive the letter inviting him to participate in the program. They are incredibly frustrated and believe the school inaccurately identified him for the program and are concerned about the other assumptions his teachers may be making based on his ethnicity. How do you respond?

Scenario 5: You have been Student E's school counselor since her freshman year. Each time you have met with her, you have discussed her desire to go to a four-year college and study political science. She has been taking rigorous coursework each year and has done very well. In a college planning meeting with her in the fall of her junior year, she shares with you that she wishes to drop her Advanced Placement courses because her father has told her that she will remain at home helping to care for her younger siblings until she is married. Although Student E wishes to attend college, she states she must accept her family's decision. What are your recommendations?

CULTURAL PROFICIENCY ENHANCEMENT

In reviewing your responses and reflections to this chapter, you have likely identified some areas for professional growth. The following Cultural Proficiency Enhancement Plan will help you determine how to refine your culturally proficient leadership skills to work for equitable outcomes. You may incorporate what you identify in this activity into the Visionary Leadership Development Plan outlined in chapter one. Once you have identified your enhancement plan, consider the resources provided at the end of this book to continue to build your cultural proficiency.

ACTIVITY: Cultural Proficiency Enhancement Plan

Figure 6.3

Name: Date:

What areas do you need to address to build your skills, knowledge or practices as a culturally proficient leader?

What resources exist in your school or district to support your development as a culturally proficient leader?

What actions can you take to build your skills and knowledge to enhance your culturally proficient practices?

What is one action you will commit to do within the next three months?

REFERENCES

American School Counselor Association. (2010). *Ethical standards for school counselors.* Retrieved from http://www.schoolcounselor.org/files/EthicalStandards2010.pdf.

American School Counselor Association (2012). *The ASCA National Model: A framework for school counseling programs* (3rd ed.). Alexandria, VA: Author.

Arredondo, P., Toporek, M. S., Brown, S., Jones, J., Locke, D. C., Sanchez, J., & Stadler, H. (1996). *Operationalization of the Multicultural Counseling Competencies.* Alexandria, VA: Association of Multicultural Counseling and Development

Bryan, J., & Henry, L., (2011) A model for building school-family-community partnerships: Principles and process. *Journal of Counseling and Development, 90,* 4.

College Board. (2007). The college keys compact. Getting ready, getting in, and getting through college: Expanding options for low-income students. New York: Author.

Cross T., Bazron, B., Dennis, K., & Isaacs, M. (1989). *Towards a culturally competent system of care, volume I.* Washington, D.C.: Georgetown University Child Development Center, CASSP Technical Assistance Center.

Grothaus, T. (2012). Multiculturalism and the ASCA National Model. In *ASCA National Model: A framework for school counseling programs* (3rd ed.; pp.14-16). Alexandria, VA: American School Counselor Association.

Grothaus, T. (2012). *Making diversity work.* Alexandria, VA: American School Counselor Association.

Hatch, T. (2012). Advocacy and social justice. In *ASCA National Model: A framework for school counseling programs* (3rd ed.; pp. 14-16). Alexandria, VA: American School Counselor Association.

Holcomb-McCoy, C., & Myers, J. E. (1999). Multicultural competence and counselor training: A national survey. *Journal of Counseling and Development, 77,* 294-302.

Holcomb-McCoy, C. (2005). Investigating school counselors' perceived multicultural competence. *Professional School Counseling. 8,* 5, 414-423.

Holcomb-McCoy, C., & Chen-Hayes, S. F. (2011). Culturally competent school counselors: Affirming diversity by challenging oppression. In B. T. Erford (Ed.), *Transforming the school counseling profession* (3rd ed., pp. 90-109). Boston: Pearson.

Lindsey, R., Robins, K. J. N., & Terrell, R. D. (2009). *Cultural proficiency: A manual for school leaders.* Thousand Oaks, CA: Corwin.

Lindsey, R. B., Roberts, L. M., & CampbellJones, F. (2005). *The culturally proficient school: An implementation guide for school leaders.* Thousand Oaks, CA: Corwin.

National Association for College Admission Counseling (2000). Statement on counselor competencies. http://www.nacacnet.org/about/Governance/Policies/Documents/CounselorCompetencies.pdf.

National Center for Education Statistics (2010). Closer look 2010: High poverty schools. http://nces.ed.gov/programs/coe/analysis/2010-section3b.asp.

National Center for Education Statistics (2012). The condition of education. http://nces.ed.gov/programs/coe/indicator_pgr.asp.

Reeves, D. B. (2008). *The leader's guide to standards: A blueprint for educational equity and Excellence.* San Francisco: Jossey-Bass.

Singleton, G. E. & Linton, C. (2006). *Courageous conversations about race: A field guide for achieving equity in schools.* Thousand Oaks, CA: Corwin.

Stephens, D. L., & Lindsey, Randall, B. (2011). *Culturally proficient collaboration: Use and misuse of school counselors.* Thousand Oaks, CA: Corwin.

Terrell, R. D., & Lindsey, R. (2008). *Culturally proficient leadership: The personal journey begins within.* Thousand Oaks, CA: Corwin.

CHAPTER 7

A Framework for District and State Leadership

"It is not fair to ask of others what you are not willing to do yourself."
Eleanor Roosevelt

State and district school counselor leaders (supervisors and directors) have the tremendous responsibility of serving as the voice for the school counselors they represent as well as developing leadership within the profession. They are charged with positioning school counseling programs to do the work necessary for student achievement, which means removing barriers for school counseling programs and professionals (ASCA, 2012). Supervisors must effectively navigate through systems to influence key decision makers by demonstrating the impact of school counseling programs and promoting the role of the school counselor as crucial to the academic achievement and success of all students.

Supervisors may face the challenge of overseeing a number of programs and services coupled with limited role-specific training and support for their positions. Frequently, they are the only one in their position within the district or state and must reach outside of their work setting to access role-specific professional development and consultation. They may or may not have a background in school counseling; thus, we provide a framework aligned with the ASCA National Model and the five school counselor leadership characteristics, as discussed in chapter three, that can be used by vertical leaders, regardless of their setting or background, to guide and support their work.

GETTING STARTED

Supervisors support school counseling programs through leadership, advocacy, collaboration and systemic change. In this chapter, we examine each of these actions and how they affect the delivery of comprehensive school counseling programs. Although supervisors serve as a voice for school counseling programs, they are frequently removed from the day-to-day operations and must find ways to connect their decisions to actions that meet the needs of those they serve. Prior to examining the framework for district and state leadership, use the following school counseling district or state program assessment activity, which aligns with the ASCA National Model school counseling program assessment, to identify areas where you feel most knowledgeable about the school counseling programs in your district or state and where you need additional information to support your work as a vertical leader.

ACTIVITY: **School Counseling District or State Program Assessment**

Complete the following assessment. For each of the statements representing elements of a comprehensive program, identify if the statement is true of the work in your district or state (yes), not occurring or not occurring consistently in your district or state (no), or if you are unsure of how this statement represents your district or state school counseling programs (unsure). For each statement, identify the data source you are using to assess the school counseling programs. If you are unsure, identify a potential data source to gather this information. Once you have completed the chart, answer the reflective questions.

Figure 7.1 School Counseling District or State Program Assessment

	Yes	No	Unknown	Data Source
FOUNDATION				
School counseling programs have clearly defined beliefs, mission and vision statements.				
School counseling programs have SMART program goals based on school data.				
School counseling program goals focus on improving achievement, attendance, behavior or school safety through the school counseling domains (academic, career and personal/social).				
Grade-specific competencies are clearly defined and based on ASCA Student Standards, state standards and other relevant student standards.				
School counselors know and abide by the ethical standards as well as state and district policies.				

	Yes	No	Unknown	Data Source
School counselors have access to the necessary resources and professional development to build professional competencies.				
School counselors have access to leadership development opportunities.				
MANAGEMENT				
School administrators and policy makers are aware of appropriate and inappropriate school counseling activities.				
School counselors spend at least 80 percent of their time in direct and indirect student services.				
Principals understand and agree to the focus of the school counseling program at their school each year.				
School counseling programs use stakeholder input to advise on program implementation.				
School counselors are proficient in the collection, analysis and interpretation of student data.				
School counselors have access to necessary data and use it to drive their programs and monitor student progress.				
School counseling programs have a plan for how they will accomplish goals.				
School counselors can develop classroom lessons using instructional best practices.				
Parents, students and the school community are aware of the school counseling program calendar.				

	Yes	No	Unknown	Data Source
DELIVERY				
School counselors have the skills to deliver classroom lessons using instructional best practices.				
School counselors have the skills necessary to run small-group counseling sessions and access to students for participation.				
School counselors monitor students' academic progress.				
School counselors are able to effectively respond to crises within their school.				
School counselors are aware of community resources supporting students and families.				
ACCOUNTABILITY				
School counselors use data to inform their programs.				
Students are assessed on the standards, and additional supports and resources are provided to students who have not yet mastered the standards.				
School counselors generate and share results reports.				
School counselor evaluation is aligned to comprehensive program expectations.				

School Counseling Program Assessment Activity Reflective Questions

1. In what areas do you have a solid understanding of the work school counseling programs are doing in your district or state?

2. In what areas do you need additional data to better inform your decision making?

3. For those items checked with a "no," what factors may be contributing to the items not placed in the "yes" column? How might you address those factors?

LEADERSHIP

(Interpersonal Influence and Professional Efficacy)
Supervisors provide leadership for school counseling programs by developing a shared vision (Levin, 2000). They are able to bring together stakeholders to build consensus around the desired outcomes for students as a result of school counseling programs. Supervisors can articulate the current realities of school counseling, and they understand what needs to happen to reach the desired state for school counseling programs based on research and best practices. They use data to drive their decision making and develop strategic plans to clearly articulate to both school counselors and the larger community the vision and goals for school counseling and how those goals will be accomplished (Kaffenberger & Young, 2013).

Supervisors endorse the alignment of school counseling standards by promoting vertical articulation between school counseling programs (Young, Millard, & Miller-Kneale, 2013). In addition to aligning preK-12 standards, vertical teaming allows preK-12 school counselors to work collaboratively to address the common needs of students and families in a community. Supervisors should work to develop district or state preK-12 standards to promote consistent expectations and outcomes for all students regardless of the schools they attend. Supervisors also view leadership as the essential element for design and implementation of comprehensive school counseling programs and are dedicated to fostering the leadership of the school counselors they support. Finally, they promote school counselors as educational leaders and provide regular leadership professional development opportunities to support the implementation of comprehensive school counseling programs. Chapter eight discusses a leadership development model that can be implemented by supervisors.

ADVOCACY

(Social Justice Advocacy)
Supervisors understand the impact of political and social influences on practice and can navigate effectively through systems as an advocate for students and school counselors. Through advocacy efforts, vertical leaders facilitate school counselors' access to the necessary tools, resources, supports, data and time with students to implement comprehensive programs supporting the success of all students. They advocate for the development of policies and practices that maximize direct and indirect services to students by sharing data showing the impact of school counseling programs on student success. Supervisors increase awareness and understanding of school counseling student standards among educational leaders and policy makers and identify how they support student success, as well as link to other content. They use ethical standards as a basis for policies addressing school counseling practices or expectations and ensure school, district and state leaders have a clear understanding of the ethical standard school counselors are expected to follow.

Although the role of the school counselor is clearly defined at the national level, it is broad and not always well understood at the school level. The district and school expectations for school counselors must continue to be monitored to prevent an unmanageable set of responsibilities. Supervisors support the retention of school counselors by promoting professional identity and informing policy decisions. This means advocating for appropriate student-to-school-counselor ratios, eliminating non-school-counseling-related responsibilities and supporting access to necessary resources and opportunities for leadership.

Supervisors promote the hiring and retention of highly effective school counselors by advocating for hiring and evaluation practices aligned with professional expectations. They provide individuals who make hiring decisions with a solid understanding of the expectations of the school counseling program and the knowledge, attitude and skills school counselors must have to implement effective programs. Supervisors may develop sample interview questions and scoring rubrics or support the hiring more directly by participating in the interview and selection process for new school counselors through recruitment fairs, candidate screening interviews or joint interviews with school-based administrators. Supervisors also work collaboratively with counselor educators to inform training that prepares students to assume school counseling roles aligned with state and district expectations. Use the following hiring and retention efforts reflective activity to examine your current practices and how they affect programs.

Hiring and Retention Efforts Reflective Activity

Using the questions below, consider your district or state's current hiring and retention efforts and their impact on school counseling programs.

Figure 7.2

1. In what ways do you support hiring that promotes comprehensive school counseling programs?

2. What do the data in your state or district suggest about your current efforts to retain highly effective school counselors?

3. Are there current practices or policies in place that do not support the hiring or retention of a diverse group of highly effective school counselors?

4. What do the data suggest you might need to do differently around hiring and retention of school counselors in your state or district?

Effective advocates are able to guide stakeholders through a discussion that makes connections between the issues and the outcomes for students, thus gaining supporters and other advocates. They understand the political landscape, how stakeholder goals and agendas align or conflict with the issue, and how to build momentum around critical issues for student success. They engage in the political process locally, at the state level and nationally to promote student success and comprehensive school counseling programs. This may include participating in parent association meetings, sharing information at school board events or lobbying at the state and national level for legislation that aids students or school counselors. Finally, supervisors know the important role they play in developing school counselors' advocacy skills to have the greatest impact on student success. They help school counselors understand how decisions affecting students are determined, how to navigate through systems, and they encourage school counselor participation in state and national associations. Use the following advocacy planning template to consider how you can best advocate for issues affecting services for students as a district or state supervisor.

Circle one of the topics below (or select one of your own) to answer the questions and determine how you would advocate on behalf of comprehensive school counseling programs.

Figure 7.3

School counselor ratios

School counselor access to students

Student access to resources

School counselor evaluations

Access to professional development

School counselor hiring practices

1. In one sentence, describe the issue and the impact on students.

2. In two to three sentences, using data, explain how this issue affects student achievement, attendance or behavior.

3. What is the desired outcome of this advocacy effort?

4. What are the existing policies or political agendas that either support or conflict with the issue?

5. Who is aware that this issue exists?

6. Who is in a position to affect this issue either directly or indirectly (with support or in opposition), and how do their values or priorities connect to this issue?

7. What are the risks and consequences (both positive and negative) in addressing this issue, and what are some ways to minimize negative consequences?

8. Is there a specific time when this issue needs to be addressed? (ex: budgeting cycle)

9. What is the key message that needs to be conveyed, and how can it be communicated?

10. Outline the steps you will take to advocate on behalf of this issue.

COLLABORATION

(Resourceful Problem-Solving and Systemic Collaboration)
Supervisors provide school counselors with the necessary resources to implement comprehensive programs. Resources include professional resources but also consist of time, financial resources, and professional consultation and collaboration. Supervisors provide professional resources to school counselors to maximize their access to evidence-based practices and minimize their need to create protocols, templates or tools that already exist or spend hours searching for frequently requested information. They engage school counselors in the selection and creation of resources and professional materials through curriculum development teams, material and software adoption processes, and online collaboration and material sharing site development. They collaborate on the content of resource handbooks to provide all school counselors with the information they need to manage district and state expectations. Following are examples of topics to include in a school counseling handbook or online resource.

Sample School Counseling Handbook or Online Resource Content
- Best practices for facilitating parent conferences
- Crisis response protocol and resources
- Community referrals
- Contact list for other school counselors and administrative offices
- Ethical guidelines
- Evaluation information
- Frequently asked questions
- preK-12 student expectations
- Policies and regulations for school counselors
- Professional development calendar
- Sample classroom lesson plans
- Sample small-group resources
- Sample school counseling brochures
- Sample results reports
- Sample SMART goals
- Tips for writing letters of recommendation

Supervisors collaborate with other leaders to negotiate time for school counselors to meet the professional expectations of the school or district. They review school counselor contract lengths, professional development and collaboration opportunities and non-school-counseling-related responsibilities preventing adequate time to support students. For example, supervisors may collaborate with principals to extend school counselor contracts to allow school counselors to support students in transition activities at the start or end of the school year. Further, supervisors secure adequate funding for school counseling programs so school counselors can purchase the necessary resources for delivery of services to students. This may include funding for site licenses for computer software for students to explore colleges and careers; securing buses for college visits; investing in technology to monitor student academic progress; or financing school counselor participation in professional workshops, conferences or webinars. Supervisors who do not have budgets to support these activities collaborate and form strategic partnerships with those who do have financial resources so money is not a barrier to comprehensive programs.

Finally, supervisors provide professional consultation and collaboration. Supervisors serve as professional consultants, and they also build opportunities for school counselors to consult and collaborate. They provide opportunities for school counselors from different schools to discuss their programs and a method for school counselors to receive meaningful feedback from peers and supervisors alike. Consultation and collaboration allow school counselors to share effective practices and exchange resources and ideas that support their work with students.

SYSTEMIC CHANGE

(Professional Efficacy)
Supervisors promote systemic change by providing school counselors with the necessary skills and knowledge to implement effective comprehensive school counseling programs addressing students' academic, college and career and personal/social needs. They support school counselors in assessing their professional competencies and developing goals and plans to address areas of personal and professional growth. They use the professional development needs of school counselors obtained through surveys or the evaluation process to create a professional development plan addressing those needs as well as the needs of the larger system. Supervisors identify ways to address needs through face-to-face trainings, virtual training, professional conferences and sharing professional articles. They consider how and when school counselors will access training and advocate for release time or additional contract time if release time will negatively affect students. Supervisors use data to assess the effectiveness of all professional development and make necessary modifications including collaborating with counselor educators when pre-service training does not align with expectations for their district or state. Finally, these vertical leaders use professional development as a leadership development opportunity by allowing school counselors to facilitate or co-facilitate trainings.

Furthermore, systemic change occurs when supervisors encourage the retention and growth of highly effective school counselors by providing professional development that promotes self-efficacy and fills skill and knowledge gaps. They are particularly aware of the importance of providing new school counselors with this professional development especially around state- or district-specific expectations. Early reports from the National Commission on Teaching and America's Future suggest that nearly 50 percent of new teachers leave the profession within their first five years (NCTAF, 2013). Although this statistic is teacher-specific, it certainly highlights the importance of investing in supports for new educators to avoid constant turnover costs and challenges. Supervisors can develop new school counselor supports such as mentoring programs, resource handbooks or induction programs. New school counselor programs also provide leadership opportunities for experienced school counselors to share their knowledge and expertise based on their reflection of needs as a new school counselor.

Implementing comprehensive school counseling programs requires school counselors to come together with a common focus as opposed to multiple school counselors in the same building operating with separate goals and foci. It is critical to the health of the school counseling program that supervisors provide professional development promoting effective teaming. Supervisors may use school counseling collaborative teams (SCCT) that follow the professional learning community model as a framework for building highly functioning school counseling teams. A highly functional SCCT provides a structure to allow school counselors to work collaboratively with norms and a cycle for continuous improvement to develop goals, plan programs and analyze data to drive decision making that results in systemic change (Young, Millard, & Miller-Kneale, 2013). Additionally, this model promotes ongoing professional development by capitalizing on the expertise of the school counselors within the building, district or area.

Professional development is critical for school counselors to ensure they have the skills and knowledge to lead comprehensive programs. Professional development plans that are built using an outcome-based model identify the desired state of school counseling programs and the skills and knowledge that must be addressed to get there. Following are sample professional development topics aligned with the four quadrants of the ASCA National Model.

Figure 7.4 Sample Professional Development Topic by Quadrant

Foundation	**Delivery**
Confidentiality and ethics	Community referrals
SMART goals	Crisis response
Leadership development	Classroom lessons
School counseling standards	Effective parent programs
	Instructional best practices
Management	**Accountability**
Action plans	Assessing student competencies
Principal/school counselor collaboration	Needs assessments
Effective advisory councils	Effective advocacy for change
Tools for disaggregating data	Results reports
	School counselor evaluations

School counseling supervisors can use leadership, advocacy, collaboration and systemic change to support school counselors in the implementation of comprehensive school counseling programs that support student achievement. Use the following district and state actions to promote comprehensive programs activity to identify those actions you are taking or will take to support comprehensive programs.

District and State Actions to Promote Comprehensive Programs Activity

For each of the four quadrants of the ASCA National Model, identify an example of leadership, advocacy, collaboration and systemic change that you provide or can provide to support school counselors in that quadrant.

Figure 7.5

	Leadership	Advocacy	Collaboration	Systemic Change
Foundation				
Management				
Delivery				
Accountability				

REFERENCES

American School Counselor Association (2012). *The ASCA National Model: A framework for school counseling programs* (3rd ed.). Alexandria, VA: Author.

Kaffenberger, C., & Young, A. (2013). *Making DATA Work* (3rd ed.). Alexandria, VA: American School Counselor Association.

Levin, I. M. (2000). Vision revisited: Telling the story of the future. *The Journal of Applied Behavioral Science, 36*, 91-107. (National Commission on Teaching and America's Future (NCTAF) http://www.nctaf.org/NCTAFWhoWillTeach.pdf.pdf). Retrieved March 1, 2013.

National Commission on Teaching and America's Future (2003). *No dream denied: A pledge to America's children.* Washington DC: Author.

Young, A., Millard, T., & Miller-Kneale, M. (2013). *Enhancing school counselor instructional leadership through collaborative teaming: Implications for principals.* National Association for Secondary School Principals (In Press).

CHAPTER 8

District Lens: A Cohort Model for Leadership Development

"Leadership should be born out of the understanding of the needs of those who would be affected by it."
Marian Anderson

School counselor district and state leaders (supervisors and directors) promote the leadership development of the school counselors they support. These vertical leaders work collaboratively with other educational leaders to create opportunities for school counselors to further their leadership skills and practices and to develop programs focused on systemically building leadership among school counselors. Although state leaders may not directly provide leadership training, they can use social justice advocacy, resourceful problem-solving, systemic collaboration, professional efficacy and interpersonal influence to create opportunities for school counselor leadership development, or they may provide leadership training and support to district leaders. For the purpose of this chapter, we will examine school counselor leadership development through a district lens; however, the considerations and suggested model can be applied in a number of contexts.

LEADERSHIP DEVELOPMENT CONSIDERATIONS

District leaders must consider a number of factors when developing leadership opportunities and programs for school counselors. First, they identify school counselors' needs, the goals and desired outcomes for leadership development activities. To identify school counselor leadership areas to enhance, district leaders can use school counselor evaluations, needs assessments or consult with principals and other school administrators who evaluate school counselors. Following are questions to consider when identifying goals for a school counselor leadership development program.

TEMPLATE School Counselor Leadership Professional Development Goal-Setting Template

Figure 8.1

Answer the following questions to identify goals for a school counselor leadership development program.

Name: Date:

1. Is the purpose of your professional development to foster vertical leadership, horizontal leadership or both?

2. What specific school counselor competencies need to be addressed during trainings?

3. What outcomes do you wish to see as a result of leadership development for school counselors?

4. How do the desired outcomes link to the school improvement goals?

5. How will you assess program effectiveness?

Once goals are identified, costs and funding are determined. The budget necessary to provide leadership development varies greatly depending on the program's goals and the existing internal resources. In analyzing financial costs, keep in mind that the time spent coordinating and delivering leadership development activities is a cost consideration as well. District leaders who make leadership development a priority should appropriate their time accordingly, which may mean abandoning other projects or programs. It is, therefore, critically important for district leaders to have the support of their supervisors and the district. The following Professional Development Budget Planning Worksheet provides a template for considering costs associated with a leadership development program.

TEMPLATE **Professional Development Budget Planning Worksheet**

Use the items below to determine costs associated with your leadership development program.

Figure 8.2

Item	Itemized Cost	# of Sessions	# of Participants	Total Cost
Building usage fees				
Consultants (speaker fees/honorariums)				
Technology resources				
Instructional resources (books, journals, etc.)				
Conference fees (local, state or national conferences)				
Materials (binders, tabs, posters, etc.)				
Food and beverages				
Printing costs				
Other				

District leaders determine a budget upfront to ensure sustainability of the program as opposed to a "one and done approach" when resources end. Federal- or state-funded grant programs, existing school district funds, private foundation grants, local community and business partners or parent association groups are all potential funding sources. It is critical that supervisors use evidence supporting the effectiveness of school counselor leadership on improving student outcomes when advocating for funding and be able to demonstrate program effectiveness.

Almost simultaneous to costs are considerations around existing internal resources available to provide leadership development for school counselors. Although some districts may have the internal staff and resources to provide leadership professional development, others may lack the capacity to provide these trainings through existing school counseling supervisory staff. If that is the case, school counseling supervisors can explore one or more of the following options:

- Work with other educators within the state or district who may have expertise and collaborate to create relevant school counselor leadership professional development.
- Partner with area counselor educators who may be willing to provide training or support at a low cost or no cost with an added benefit for action research.
- Collaborate with neighboring districts to combine efforts and resources to develop and deliver a program.
- Connect with state school counseling associations, which may be willing to provide low-cost professional development.
- Employ a professional consultant to support development and/or delivery of leadership training.

As the program becomes more clearly defined, a training model will need to be outlined addressing access to school counselors. Supervisors will need to determine if there is support to provide training during the work day or if there are funds or incentives to provide school counselors with training outside of their work schedule either on weekends, in the evenings or during the summer. The overwhelming advantage to training school counselors during their regular work schedule is the equity in access to the trainings that cannot be provided if school counselors have conflicting responsibilities outside of their school day. The major drawback to this model is certainly student, staff and parent access to the school counselor. Supervisors will need to carefully weigh the options and discuss the pros and cons with principals to solicit their support of the selected training model. Consider the questions in the following Leadership Professional Development Planning Template, which can be used in conjunction with the goal-setting template and budget worksheet to create a plan for school counselor leadership development.

Leadership Professional Development Planning Template

Consider the questions below to develop a plan for your district's school counselor leadership professional development.

Figure 8.3

1. What are the goals of the school counselor leadership professional development training, and how did you identify those goals?

2. Whose support do you need to enlist prior to providing the leadership development (ex: principals)?

3. What are the program costs, and how is it going to be funded?

4. Who will design and deliver the professional development?

5. Will the trainings be open to any school counselor who wishes to participate, or will there be a selection process or other qualifying factors?

6. Will each participant have common training, or will training be tailored to each individual school counselor's needs?

7. When, how often and over what span of time will professional development occur?

8. How will the program be evaluated?

COHORT MODEL FOR SCHOOL COUNSELOR LEADERSHIP DEVELOPMENT

Although a variety of leadership development models exist, we present a school counselor leadership cohort (SCLC) model that can be considered to build school counselor leadership capacity. A cohort model for leadership development honors the skills and knowledge each member brings to a group, allowing participants to learn from the facilitator as well as each other (Lambert, 2003). As opposed to instructor-focused professional development, there is an expectation that cohort members actively participate in the learning process by providing insights and sharing their experiences and knowledge with the group. Learning is most powerful when participants have similar outcome goals and thus build a sense of community and mutual responsibility for learning. Cohorts require a commitment over time, and this model is most effective when no more than 20 individuals are invited or selected to participate with a clear understanding of a cohort commitment.

COHORT MISSION, VISION AND GOALS

A cohort model can be used to build both horizontal and vertical leadership depending on participant needs and program goals. The SCLC focuses on developing the knowledge, skills and capacity of school counselors who have already demonstrated leadership potential in their current school settings, thus enhancing their horizontal leadership and preparing them to assume lead school counselor or supervisor (vertical) leadership positions. The SCLC mission, vision and goals drive the program including participant selection, activities and evaluation. The SCLC mission, vision and goals are shared when soliciting program participants; however, because each cohort is unique and the needs of each vary, some additional goals may be set once participant needs are identified.

Each cohort member sets individual leadership development goals based on desired outcomes, a self-assessment of school counselor competencies and other leadership standards that may be relevant to his or her short- and long-term goals. Cohort participants who aspire to supervisory roles may consider their professional development needs around the Interstate School Leaders Licensure Consortium (ISLLC) Standards, which are used for school leadership licensure assessments and provide a strong foundation for vertical school counselor leadership (Derrington & Sharratt, 2008).

ISLLC Standards
- **Standard 1:** A school administrator is an educational leader who promotes the success of all students by facilitating the development, articulation, implementation and stewardship of a vision of learning that is shared and supported by the school community.
- **Standard 2:** A school administrator is an educational leader who promotes the success of all students by advocating, nurturing and sustaining a school culture and instructional program conducive to student learning and staff professional growth.
- **Standard 3:** A school administrator is an educational leader who promotes the success of all students by ensuring management of the organization, operations and resources for a safe, efficient and effective learning environment.

- **Standard 4:** A school administrator is an educational leader who promotes the success of all students by collaborating with families and community members, responding to diverse community interests and needs and mobilizing community resources.
- **Standard 5:** A school administrator is an educational leader who promotes the success of all students by acting with integrity, fairness and in an ethical manner.
- **Standard 6:** A school administrator is an educational leader who promotes the success of all students by understanding, responding to and influencing the larger political, social, economic, legal and cultural context.

Once cohort participants identify their individual goals and leadership development needs, they provide information to cohort facilitators to help guide the program activities. In the case of the SCLC, these activities occur monthly over the course of a school year. The following Leadership Development Template provides a framework for capturing individual cohort members' learning needs and leadership goals.

Sample Leadership Development Template

School counseling cohort members can use this template to identify their professional learning needs and leadership goals.

Figure 8.4

Name: Date:

1. What are your short- and long-term leadership goals?

2. What are your existing leadership strengths based on relevant standards?

3. What leadership skills do you want to develop this year?

4. What opportunities will you seek out to develop those skills?

5. How will you use your leadership skills to have an impact on student success?

IDENTIFYING COHORT PARTICIPANTS

When developing a cohort, supervisors must consider the composition and size of the program. It is also critical to revisit the program goals and vision to identify appropriate candidates. Principal support is vital when selecting candidates as it ensures support for school counselor participation and also lends credibility to the program. Cohort participants can be invited to participate through a nomination process where they are identified by a vertical leader such as a principal in the school system and guaranteed a place in the cohort or through an application process. If candidates are selected through an application process, the application should clearly state the program purpose, requirements, selection criteria and the application deadline. In addition to capturing basic demographic information, the application may also provide candidates with an opportunity to demonstrate their ability to communicate effectively in writing through a cover letter and/or a writing sample. A writing sample or cover letter can provide a sense of how closely the candidate's goals are aligned to the cohort goals and mission by gathering additional information about their leadership perspective and vision for school counseling. An application should also include letters of recommendation reflecting the candidate's existing leadership capacity.

The SCLC uses an application process to select highly qualified and motivated candidates who bring with them diverse perspectives and experiences and can provide insights that will help shape the learning process for themselves and their colleagues. Because the SCLC includes monthly sessions during the school day and beyond the work day, the SCLC application process includes essays, supervisor endorsement, two letters of recommendation and an interview process to identify applicants who will be able to fulfill cohort expectations. A selection committee composed of vertical leaders who have a clear understanding of comprehensive school counseling programs and the mission of the cohort reviews applications and selects the strongest candidates to participate in a panel interview. A sample application packet, writing prompts and interview questions are provided in Appendix B.

Final acceptance decisions are shared with both SCLC applicants and their supervisors, and those who are not selected are provided with an opportunity to receive feedback on their application to support their continued professional growth and leadership development and strengthen their candidacy should they choose to apply to the cohort in subsequent years. The following Cohort Selection Considerations Template provides questions for supervisors to consider when determining how they will identify cohort participants.

TEMPLATE **Cohort Selection Considerations Template**

Use the following template to identify criteria for cohort participation.

Figure 8.5

1. What is the ideal cohort size based on desired results and current funding support?

2. Will there be a minimum number of years of experience as a school counselor required to participate in the program?

3. Will the cohort serve school counselors in all settings (elementary, middle, high, alternative schools, etc.) concurrently, or will a specific group be targeted?

4. What form of advertisement will be used to market the program or share information about the cohort in advance of selecting candidates?

5. Will participants be identified through an application process or through a nomination process?

   a. If participants are identified through a nomination process, who will do the nominating?

   b. If participants are selected through an application process, will all candidates who apply be accepted? If not, who will select the candidates?

6. If prospective candidates are not selected for the cohort, what type of feedback and opportunities will be provided to them to support their professional development?

COHORT ACTIVITIES AND TOPICS

Cohorts address various topics, and members may participate in a range of activities based on the program goals, the number of sessions and the needs of the participants. The SCLC meets once a month for seven full-day trainings over the course of the school year. Each month focuses on a different area of leadership that supports school counselors in expanding their horizontal and vertical leadership capacity. Woven throughout the cohort are opportunities to engage in professional reading, group discussions and reflective writing to support individual growth and goals. Cohort members are also encouraged to participate in professional development activities outside of the program and are required to lead a professional development session in collaboration with other cohort members for school counselors in the district.

The first month of the cohort focuses on participants gaining a more clear understanding of leadership and their own leadership strengths and areas for growth to build personal efficacy. Month two provides participants with opportunities to understand leadership in context and enhance their knowledge of navigating through a system as a leader by shadowing vertical leaders within the district and engaging experienced leaders through a leadership panel discussion. The third month concentrates on accountability and resourceful problem-solving. As a part of this focus, participants identify an achievement gap issue within their school and focus on that issue throughout the year. They use data to identify the gap, inform interventions, advocate for resources and monitor the effectiveness in closing the gap.

Month four focuses on equity and cultural proficiency, and participants are provided with advocacy training addressing achievement gaps and ensuring equity and access. The fifth session spotlights the skills necessary to lead change by examining interpersonal influence. Session six allows participants to explore vertical leadership by highlighting hiring and supervision issues and developing interview and resume-writing skills. The final cohort meeting synthesizes cohort member learning as members present their accountability projects to vertical leaders throughout the district and reflect on learning and next steps (Linn, Gill, Sherman, Vaughn, Mixon, 2010). Following is sample monthly calendar for a leadership cohort. Athough the cohort focuses on leadership development, an essential goal is to build a support network for aspiring leaders. Cohort members become trusted confidants with a shared commitment to equity for students. They continue their professional growth as a cohort well after the conclusion of the monthly meetings.

Leadership Cohort Sample Monthly Calendar

Month 1: Exploring Leadership (Personal Efficacy)
- Leadership models
- Individual leadership strengths
- Leadership development plan

Month 2: Leadership in Context (Systemic Collaboration)
- Q&A panel with experienced leaders
- Leadership shadowing

Month 3: Leading for Outcomes (Resourceful Problem-Solving)
- School counselor accountability
- Understanding college and career readiness

Month 4: Leading for Equity (Social Justice Advocacy)
- Understanding achievement gaps
- Cultural proficiency
- Advocacy

Month 5: Leading Change (Interpersonal Influence)
- Strategic planning
- Communication strategies
- Managing conflict

Month 6: Preparing for Vertical Leadership Positions
- Supervising and evaluating staff
- Resume writing
- Interview preparation

Month 7: Leadership Reflections
- Cohort project presentations
- Cohort reflections
- Cohort evaluation

COHORT EVALUATION

Evaluation is a critical aspect of determining program effectiveness. School counseling supervisors should collect both formative and summative data to determine the effectiveness of their program as well as to make program adjustments as needed (ASCA, 2012; Gusky, 2000; Killion, 2008). Cohort participants can provide perception data through pre and post assessments or exit slips to provide insight into the effectiveness of each activity. Exit slips are used as prompts to (a) provide formative assessment data, (b) stimulate self-analysis, (c) focus on instructional strategies or (d) enhance open communication (Marzano, 2012, p. 80). Additionally, a final program evaluation should be conducted to gather summative data. A sample program evaluation is available in Appendix B.

SELF-DIRECTED LEADERSHIP DEVELOPMENT ACTIVITIES

In the absence of formal leadership cohorts or training, school counselors can still create their own plan for leadership development and seek opportunities to build their horizontal and vertical leadership capacity. For example, they may serve as a supervisor for graduate students or mentor a new school counselor. They can author professional articles or develop school counseling curriculum for their district. School counselors may develop a training session for their professional colleagues or present at a state, regional or national conference. They can serve on school improvement planning teams or volunteer for state or district initiatives. School counselors can initiate contact with leaders in their district or state to arrange job shadowing experiences or participate in resume writing or interviewing workshops held in their community. There are numerous opportunities for school counselors to build leadership capacity. A willingness to go beyond expectations and work outside of your current capacity can support professional learning and growth. Examples of self-directed leadership activities, including associated costs, time commitments and leadership capacity built, follow. As you review this list, think about other opportunities that may exist.

Sample Self-Directed Leadership Activities and Associated Costs

Activity	Potential Costs	Participant Time Commitment	Horizontal Leadership	Vertical Leadership
Leadership shadowing	Travel	Low	X	X
Complete the leadership development template in this chapter	None	Low	X	X
Present at a state, district, regional or national conference	Travel	Moderate	X	X
Mentor new school counselors	Travel	Moderate	X	X
Supervise school counseling graduate students	None	High	X	X
Author a professional article	None	High	X	X
Attend a resume writing workshop	None	Moderate		X
Participate in a mock interview	None	Low		X

Activity	Potential Costs	Participant Time Commitment	Horizontal Leadership	Vertical Leadership
Serve on the school planning team	None	High	X	X
Serve on a state or district initiative	Travel	High	X	X
Develop curriculum	Supplies	High	X	X
Serve on a committee or in a leadership position for the state school counseling association	Travel	Moderate to High	X	X

SCHOOL COUNSELOR LEADERSHIP: THE ESSENTIAL PRACTICE

School counselor leadership development is a critical focus for the development and sustainability of comprehensive school counseling programs. This book offers numerous opportunities to reflect on your personal beliefs about leadership, identify individual leadership characteristics and increase your horizontal and vertical school counselor leadership capacity. Finally, you are encouraged to:

- **L**ive your belief that all students are capable of achieving and deserve to graduate high school college- and career-ready.
- **E**xcellence is a minimum standard.
- **A**dvocate for all students.
- **D**ecide that success for all students is the only option.

REFERENCES

American School Counselor Association (2012). *The ASCA National Model: A framework for school counseling programs* (3rd. ed.). Alexandria, VA: Author.

Derrington, M. L., & Sharratt, G., (2008). Evaluation of school principals using Interstate School Leaders Licensure Consortium (ISLLC) Standards, *AASA Journal of Scholarship and Practice, 5*(3).

Gusky, T. R. (2000). *Evaluating professional development.* Thousand Oaks, CA: Corwin Press, Inc.

Killion, J. (2008). *Assessing impact: Evaluating staff development.* Thousand Oaks, CA: Corwin Press.

Lambert, L. (2003). *Leadership capacity for lasting school improvement.* Alexandria: Association for Supervision and Curriculum Development.

Linn, G. B., Gill, P., Sherman, R., Vaughn, G., & Mixon, J. (2010). Evaluating the long-term impact of professional development. *Professional Development in Education, 36,* 679-682. doi: 10.1080/19415250903109288.

Marzano, R. (2012). The many uses of exit slips. *Educational Leadership, 70,* 2, 80-81.

MULTICULTURAL COUNSELING COMPETENCE AND TRAINING SURVEY-REVISED

Multicultural Counseling Competence Component
(School Counselor Version)

Developed by Cheryl Holcomb-McCoy, Ph.D.
The Johns Hopkins University

Directions: Listed below are competency statements based on the Association of Multicultural Counseling and Development's Multicultural Counseling Competencies and Explanatory Statements. Please read each competency statement, and evaluate your multicultural competence using the following four-point scale.

1 - **Not competent (Not able to perform at this time)**
2 - **Somewhat competent (More training needed)**
3 - **Competent (Able to perform competently)**
4 - **Extremely competent (Able to perform at a high level)**

1. I can discuss my own ethnic/cultural heritage. 1 2 3 4

2. I am aware of how my cultural background and experiences have influenced my attitudes about psychological processes. 1 2 3 4

3. I am able to discuss how my culture has influenced the way I think. 1 2 3 4

4. I can recognize when my attitudes, beliefs and values are interfering with providing the best services to my students. 1 2 3 4

5. I verbally communicate my acceptance of culturally different students. 1 2 3 4

6. I nonverbally communicate my acceptance of culturally different students. 1 2 3 4

7. I can discuss my family's perspective regarding acceptable and nonacceptable codes of conduct. 1 2 3 4

8. I can discuss models of white racial identity development. 1 2 3 4

9. I can define racism. 1 2 3 4

10. I can define prejudice. 1 2 3 4

11. I can define discrimination. 1 2 3 4

12. I can define stereotype. 1 2 3 4

13. I can identify the cultural bases of my communication style. 1 2 3 4

14. I can identify my negative and positive emotional reactions toward persons of other racial and ethnic groups. 1 2 3 4

15. I can identify my reactions that are based on stereotypical belief about different ethnic groups. 1 2 3 4

16. I can give examples of how stereotypical beliefs about culturally different persons impact the counseling relationship. 1 2 3 4

17. I can articulate the possible differences between the nonverbal behavior of the five major ethnic groups (i.e., African/black, Hispanic/Latino, Asian, Native American, European/white). 1 2 3 4

18. I can articulate the possible differences between the verbal behavior of the five major ethnic groups. 1 2 3 4

19. I can discuss the counseling implications for at least two models of racial/ethnic identity development. 1 2 3 4

20. I can discuss within-group differences among ethnic groups (e.g., low socio-economic status Puerto Rican student vs. high socio-economic status Puerto Rican student). 1 2 3 4

21. I can discuss how culture affects a student's vocational choices. 1 2 3 4

22. I can discuss how culture affects the help-seeking behaviors of students. 1 2 3 4

23. I can discuss how culture affects the manifestations of psychological disorders. 1 2 3 4

24. I can describe the degree to which a counseling approach is appropriate for a specific group of people. 1 2 3 4

25. I can explain how factors such as poverty and powerlessness have influenced the current conditions of at least two ethnic groups. 1 2 3 4

26. I can discuss research regarding mental health issues among culturally/ethnically different populations. 1 2 3 4

27. I can discuss how the counseling process may conflict with the cultural values of at least two ethnic groups. 1 2 3 4

28. I can list at least three barriers that prevent ethnic minority students from using counseling services. 1 2 3 4

29. I can discuss the potential bias of two assessment instruments frequently used in the schools.   1 2 3 **4**

30. I can discuss family counseling from a cultural/ethnic perspective.   1 2 3 **4**

31. I can anticipate when my helping style is inappropriate for a culturally different student.   1 2 3 **4**

32. I can help students determine whether a problem stems from racism or biases in others.   1 2 3 **4**

Reprinted with permission, Holcomb-McCoy (2005)

Scoring the MCCTS-R (Revised 6/05)

To score the competence scale of the MCCTS-R, sum the items for each of the three multicultural competence factors below.

Factor 1: Multicultural Terminology: Items 9-12

Factor 2: Multicultural Knowledge: Items 8, 13, 16-32

Factor 3: Multicultural Awareness: Items 1-7, 14-15

Sum the items for each factor. Next, compute the average score for each factor. Higher scores denote higher perceived multicultural competence.

SAMPLE COHORT APPLICATION

The purpose of the leadership cohort is to further develop school counselors' leadership capacity and promote the implementation of ASCA National Model-based school counseling programs. To be considered, applicants must have at least three years of experience working as a school counselor and have demonstrated leadership and the potential to lead comprehensive school counseling programs promoting college and career readiness and student success. The completed application packet must be submitted no later than (date) to the district school counseling office. Questions can be directed to the district school counseling office at (phone).

Name: _____

Address: _____

Phone numbers: _____

E-mail: _____

Current school: _____

Years of school counseling experience: _____

Cover Letter and Resume
Attach a current resume and cover letter highlighting your professional experiences and addressing how you plan to use the skills gained from the cohort.

Recommendations
Your application must include two letters of recommendation, one of which must be from your principal. Please submit both letters in a sealed envelope.

Principal's Endorsement
I wish to be considered as a candidate for the School Counselor Leadership Cohort. I understand that the first step of eligibility is to have the endorsement of my principal. I realize participation means I will be away from my school once a month for meetings and will be unavailable to students, parents and staff that day. Additionally, I understand I am expected to participate in a full-day job shadowing experience, complete a leadership book review and participate in the district leadership conference. In submitting this application, I am committing myself to this work as well as my work as a professional school counselor.

_____

Applicant's signature

I support the candidacy of _____
for the School Counselor Leadership Cohort.

Principal's signature:_____ Date _____

SAMPLE COHORT RECOMMENDATION FORM

Name and title of person completing this form: _____

Phone: _____ E-mail: _____

Relationship to applicant: _____

How long have you known this applicant: _____

_____ is applying for the School Counselor Leadership Cohort. The purpose of the cohort is to further develop the leadership capacity of school counselors to promote the implementation of ASCA National Model-based school counseling programs. To be considered, applicants must have at least three years of experience working as a school counselor and have demonstrated leadership and the potential to lead comprehensive school counseling programs promoting college and career readiness and student success.

Compared with other school counselors you have encountered, please rate the candidate based on the following characteristics or practices:

	Top 1%	Outstanding (top 5%)	Excellent (top 10%)	Above Average	Average	Below Average	No Basis
Leadership							
Accomplishes goals							
Collaboration							
Visionary thinker							
Resourceful problem solver							
Promotes positive change							
Professionalism							
Advocacy							
Makes data-driven decisions							
Integrity							
Motivates others							
Reaction to setbacks							
Navigates system politics							
Responds to inequities							
Overall rating							

SAMPLE APPLICATION WRITING PROMPTS

1. As a leader, how do you use data to support student success?

2. Leaders are confronted with difficult situations every day. Write about a time when you were confronted with a difficult situation, and share how you addressed it.

3. If you could build and lead the ideal school counseling program, what would it look like?

SAMPLE COHORT INTERVIEW QUESTIONS

1. Please tell us why you are applying to the School Counselor Leadership Cohort.

2. Provide an example of a social justice issue you have confronted as a school counselor. What did you do to address the situation at the time, and what might you have done differently?

3. Describe a time where you have engaged multiple stakeholders to accomplish a goal. How did you gain stakeholder buy-in, and what might you do differently when working with stakeholders in the future?

4. Discuss how you use data to assess the effectiveness of your school counseling program and plan for student success?

5. As a leader in school counseling, how will you work to close the achievement gap?

SAMPLE COHORT EVALUATION

Provide us with your perceptions of how the School Counselor Leadership Cohort supported your leadership development. This is an anonymous survey, and responses will be used to inform development of future programs. Please rate the following statements as a result of your participation in the cohort.

	Strongly Disagree	Disagree	Neutral	Agree	Strongly Agree
I believe I have the skills to lead comprehensive school counseling programs.					
I understand how to navigate through our school system and community to secure resources for students.					
I use accountability measures to support college and career readiness for all students.					
I understand schoolwide and districtwide priorities and align my work with those goals.					
I engage stakeholders to accomplish goals.					
I share my innovative ideas.					
I can build a strategic plan.					
I advocate for students by challenging the status quo.					
I remain calm in the face of adversity.					
I understand my leadership strengths and use them to accomplish goals and inspire others.					
Cohort sessions were informative and presented information that was new to me.					
Cohort presenters were knowledgeable and prepared.					
The cohort topics were interesting and connected to my work as a school counselor leader.					
I was able to meet the goals I established at the start of the cohort.					

ADDITIONAL RESOURCES

Web Sources
Achieve *www.achieve.org*
ALLTHINGSPLC *www.allthingsplc.info/*
America's Promise Alliance *www.americaspromise.org/*
ASCD *www.ascd.org*
American School Counselor Association *www.schoolcounselor.org*
ASCA Scene *www.schoolcounselor.groupsite.com*
Career Readiness Partner Council *www.careerreadynow.org/*
Center for Creative Leadership *www.ccl.org/Leadership*
Center for Excellence in School Counseling and Leadership *www.cescal.org/*
Center for Leadership and Educational Equity *http://leadershipandequity.org/*
Center for School Counseling Outcome Research and Evaluation
    www.umass.edu/schoolcounseling
Complete College America *http://completecollege.org*
Education Trust *www.edtrust.org*
GovTrack *www.govtrack.us/*
Leading Success *www.leadingsuccess.org*
National Association for College Admission Counseling *www.nacacnet.org*
National Association of Elementary School Principals *www.naesp.org*
National Association of Secondary School Principals *www.principals.org*
National Center for Education Statistics *http://nces.ed.gov/*
National Office for School Counselor Advocacy *www.nosca.collegeboard.org*

Recommended Leadership Books
Five Dysfunctions of a Team: A Leadership Fable (Patrick Lencioni)
High Fliers: Developing the Next Generation of Leaders (Morgan W. McCall, Jr.)
Leading Everyday: 124 Actions for Effective Leadership (Joyce Kaser, Susan Mundry,
    Katherine Stiles, & Susan Loucks-Horsley)
Leadership 2.0 (Travis Bradberry & jean Greaves)
Leadership and Sustainability (Michael Fullan)
Leadership on the Line: Staying Alive through the Dangers of Leading- Ronald A. Heifetz
    & Marty Linsky
Leadership Theory and Practice (Peter Northouse)
Learning by Doing (Richard Dufour, Rebecca Dufour, Robert Eaker, & Thomas Many)
The Leadership Challenge: How to Make Extraordinary Things Happens in Organizations
    (James M. Kouzes & Barry Posner)
The Learning Leader (Douglas Reeves)
The 21 Irrefutable Laws of Leadership: Follow them and People Will Follow You
    (John Maxwell)
The Moral Imperative of School Leadership (Michael Fullan)
School Leadership: Handbook for Excellence in Student Learning (Bambrick Santoyo &
    Doug Lemov)
Simplifying Response to Intervention (Austin Buffum, Mike Mattos & Chris Weber)

ABOUT THE AUTHORS

Anita Young, Ph.D., is an assistant professor at Johns Hopkins University. She has approximately 20 years of experience in the school counseling profession as a school counselor, school-based director of student services and district school counseling supervisor. As a district school counseling supervisor, she led the charge to transform traditional school counseling services to data-driven comprehensive school counseling programs through the development of leadership cohort models. Her fundamental beliefs that all students can achieve drive her research interests to examine data outcomes that close achievement gaps and practices that cultivate school counselor leadership. She has served on numerous state, regional and national school counseling boards and councils. She is also the co-author of "Making DATA Work" and numerous journal articles.

Marcy Miller-Kneale is the coordinator for school counseling and college success for Fairfax County Public Schools in Fairfax, Va. She began her career in education with the Head Start Program and believes school, community and family partnerships are critical to the success of students. She has worked with students in grades preK-12 as a school counselor and director of student services. In 2009, prior to her work in the district office, her high school received the Recognized ASCA Model Program designation. Her research interests relate to increasing school counselor leadership capacity and developing and analyzing policies that promote college and career readiness for all students.